BOOK SELECTION AND

THE H. W. WILSON COMPANY   1970

NTELLECTUAL FREEDOM

LeRoy Charles Merritt

Dean School of Librarianship University of Oregon

BOOK SELECTION AND INTELLECTUAL FREEDOM

Copyright © 1970

Mary L. Merritt, Executor, Estate of LeRoy Charles Merritt

International Standard Book Number 0-8242-0420-4

Library of Congress Catalog Card Number 79-116998

PRINTED IN THE UNITED STATES OF AMERICA

For Mary

Who has helped immeasurably to crystallize the
convictions from which these pages are written.

PREFACE

In a very real sense, the genesis of this volume goes back to the publication in 1955 of *Public Libraries Division Reporter* No. 4, which reported the proceedings of a work conference on book selection policies at the Philadelphia conference of the American Library Association and may be considered, apart from the Library Bill of Rights, as the first significant ALA publication in the general area of book selection and intellectual freedom. That issue of the *Reporter* constituted a synthesis of the thinking of the large number of people who participated in the conference. Though never brought together as a group, a similarly large number of people have contributed to the content of the present work, many of them inadvertently, as they confronted the tendencies toward censorship to the best of their knowledge and ability.

The immediate impetus for this monograph was a 1962 letter from Mrs. Ruth M. White, then assistant to the Executive Secretary of the Public Library Association, who was in search of an author for a new *Public Libraries Division Reporter* in the same general area as No. 4, which had gone out of print. Her letter reads in part:

> I would hope that the *Reporter* could do three things: (1) give some examples of good book selection policies (at least the paragraphs relating to selection of fiction and controversial subjects) and supporting statements, (2) present case histories or background on several types of attacks with more effective ways of counteracting the pressure groups, and (3) present recommendations to all libraries, but especially public libraries, on the preparation before trouble comes and on the best procedures after trouble has arrived.

Considerably augmented, two of these three areas constitute the present volume. The case studies were omitted because of potential redundancy with other recent works and because of their tendency to become dated.

The assistance of librarians known to be interested in the problem was sought at a planning conference during the 1963 Midwinter Meeting in Chicago, and more extensively during the following spring. Response was immediate, cordial, helpful, and in some part contradictory. We could not have wanted or expected it to be otherwise. Though those who contributed counsel and suggestions are too numerous to name, my gratitude and thanks go equally to all. Similar grateful thanks go to the librarians and administrators who developed the book selection policies abstracted and recorded in Chapter 3. For the selection of the content of this chapter, and for the remainder of the volume, the author alone is responsible, and he realizes full well that he could not have written his portion without the benefit of the previous experience and writing of his colleagues in the field of intellectual freedom.

LeRoy Charles Merritt
March 1970

TABLE OF CONTENTS

PREFACE   7

1   Book Selection and
     Intellectual Freedom   11

2   Writing a
     Selection Policy   24

3   Sample
     Selection Policies   32
    I.   Adult Book Selection Policy   33
   II.   Young Adult Book Selection Policy   50
  III.   Children's Book Selection Policy   52

4 Evaluating the
        Policy   55

5 The Role of Professional Associations
        and State Library Agencies   64

6 Professional Activity in Behalf of
        Intellectual Freedom   71

APPENDIX   Basic Documents   82
            1. Library Bill of Rights   82
            2. Resolution on Loyalty Programs   83
            3. Statement on Labeling   83
            4. Freedom to Read Statement   84
            5. School Library Bill of Rights   88
            6. How Libraries and Schools Can
                 Resist Censorship   89
            7. Citizen's Request for Reconsideration
                 of a Book   91
            8. Intellectual Freedom in Libraries   92

BIBLIOGRAPHY   94

INDEX   97

CHAPTER 1

BOOK SELECTION
AND INTELLECTUAL FREEDOM

In very general terms, it may be said that there are two theories of public library book selection which are almost as diametrically opposed to each other as the two poles. Too simply, perhaps, they may be designated as the value theory and the demand theory. The value theory posits the public library as an educational institution containing books that provide inspiration, information, and recreation, with insistence that even the last-mentioned should embody some measure of creative imagination. The collection should include only those books which one way or another tend toward the development and enrichment of life. In short, "give them what they should have."

The demand theory, on the other hand, sees the public library as a democratic institution, supported by taxes paid by the whole community, each member of which has an equal right to find what he wishes to read in the library collection. In short, "give them what they want." Just as no man can live well or for long at either pole, so no librarian can espouse either the value theory or the demand theory to the exclusion of the other. Nor is life on the equator especially salutary or easily possible. So it is that each librarian works out some sort of "temperate" compromise, and if all goes well, his library acquires and holds a clientele which is comfortable with the collection it finds.

The relative weight of the two theories varies from field to field within a given library, varies somewhat between libraries of the same type, and may vary greatly between different types of libraries. In the context of intellectual freedom, the librarian needs to be in the position of being able to argue for the value of his collection to his community and, by corollary, for the place of every book in that collection as being of value to some group of readers in the community.

Acting in good conscience and without fear of intimidation, the librarian must select each book as being in fact a positive contribution to the collection and of potential benefit or usefulness to some portion of the library's clientele. He must select each book not because it will do no harm but because it may do some good. There is an important corollary to this. A book is selected because of its usefulness to a group of readers, even though it may not be useful to others, or may even be distasteful, repugnant, or objectionable to them. It is selected for its positive value to a certain group of patrons, despite the possibility of another patron's objecting or the likelihood of controversy.

It is important also that the librarian harbor no fear that he is engaging in censorship himself when a title is rejected as not belonging in the library according to established policy. The distinction made by Asheim between selection and censorship on the librarian's part [1] is a valid one and must be completely understood, felt, and believed if the librarian is to be in a proper frame of mind to withstand an onslaught from people with tendencies toward censorship. The librarian who feels, believes, or suspects that he himself engages in a measure of censorship in the process of selection is in a poor psychological position when the real thing comes, either as a request to remove a book or to add one the librarian considers unacceptable.

That some librarians consciously or unconsciously do engage in censorship in the selection process is an unfortunate irrelevancy. The

---

[1] Lester Asheim, "Not Censorship but Selection," *Wilson Library Bulletin*, 28 (September 1953), 63-67.

Fiske report,[2] with its evidence of conscious and subconscious censorship by librarians engaged in book selection, stands on its own merits. The *Newsletter on Intellectual Freedom* gives almost issue-by-issue testimony that Fiske's findings are as valid now as they were a decade ago, and not only in California but in all parts of the country. The purpose of this chapter is to assist the librarian in moving toward a firm and sound position on intellectual freedom in the selection process. The remainder of the volume is devoted to precepts, techniques, and practices which it is hoped will assist the librarian to withstand tendencies toward censorship from outside the library. This chapter is primarily concerned with those sensitive areas of book selection where librarians are divided in theory and in practice, where they find a conflict between selection theory and legal requirements, and where their selection policies and practices have been challenged.

Obscenity and Pornography. Let us begin by attempting to define the indefinable. Etymologically, *pornography*, which is derived from the Greek, means writing about prostitutes or prostitution. In common usage it is defined as meaning "a depiction (as in writing or painting) of licentiousness or lewdness: a portrayal of erotic behavior designed to cause sexual excitement." [3] The definition is clear, but it reveals that the application of the term to any work is bound to be subjective. Only the author himself can say what effect a particular work or passage in a work is "designed" to produce. What the reader concludes about the author's intentions can only be an inference.

Obscene, from the Latin, applies to whatever is indecent, disgusting, or grossly offensive, including, although not limited to, things sexual or scatological. What is considered obscene varies greatly from culture to culture, from time to time, from place to place, from art form to art form. Hardly any instrumental music could be considered obscene. Much that would be regarded as obscene if performed on stage is portrayed in books, the reading of which is essentially a private activity. This is still broadly true, even though there is now much more freedom

---

[2] Marjorie Fiske, *Book Selection and Censorship* (Berkeley: University of California Press, 1959).

[3] *Webster's Third New International Dictionary,* under "pornography," sense 2.

in regard to nudity and erotic behavior on stage and screen than would have seemed possible a generation ago.

In law, the word *obscene* may be described as indefinable. The best legal minds, including those on the Supreme Court, have labored mightily, and failed. They will continue to fail, for like beauty, obscenity is in the eye of the beholder (as noted above, *pornography* is an equally subjective term). In literature the effort at definition is just as impossible, and as pointless. Books fall above or below the level of critical acceptability according to contemporary theories and standards of literary criticism, of which obscenity is not one. A book achieves critical acceptance on criteria other than the amount or the frankness of its sexual content. A book with little or no other content fails to achieve acceptance on those same literary criteria.

So it is also with library book selection. An actual or theoretical obscenity quotient is not a criterion of selection. Neither Haines, nor Carter and Bonk, nor Ranganathan mention it. The librarian who rejects *Valley of the Dolls* or *The Arrangement* as trash is on firm literary ground; the librarian who rejects either because of its sexual content must in consistency withdraw a host of much better books from his collections. The librarian willing to work at selecting fiction and other creative writing by good literary standards will be in a sound position to defend any of his selections against charges of their alleged obscenity.

Sex Education. Broderick reported that three quarters of the public libraries buying books on sex consider it necessary to keep them in protective custody.[4] Libraries not buying such books gave as a reason that "This type material disappears from shelves." Conversely, libraries keeping the books on open shelves reported little or no theft or mutilation. Some librarians expressed annoyance that such books wear out and need to be replaced. These differences in practice can possibly be explained by differences in clientele in various parts of the country and in communities of various sizes. The more probable explanation, however, is the difference in attitude on the part of the librarians concerned. The importance of having such books in the library was disputed by none of Broderick's respondents. Considering the known reluctance on

---

[4] Dorothy Broderick, "Problem Nonfiction," *Library Journal*, 87 (October 1, 1962), 3373-8.

the part of many library patrons to ask for books on sex education, there is a correspondingly strong argument for keeping them on the open shelves. Providing for a certain amount of loss by theft must be considered part of the cost of purveying authoritative information in this sensitive area in our society.

Religion. The paragraph on religion in the composite selection policy in Chapter 3 sets forth a standard library position on the selection of religious books in the public library. The field is usually not touched on in school library selection policies, but no school library can be considered complete without the Bible and some histories of religion, both ancient and modern. Religion is a major part of our culture and can be dealt with as such without being presented as doctrine.

Not covered in public library selection policies, probably because their occurrence is rare, are the occasional books critical of a particular religion. Paul Blanshard's critical works on Roman Catholicism will serve as cases in point of books which should be in public libraries in communities where there is public interest in them. Members of a faith are not all of a piece in their attitude toward such works. Even a devout Catholic may want to know what a sincere critic has to say about his faith. The librarian need only follow the normal selection criteria for nonfiction in this sensitive area; and having thus selected such titles, he will be in a strong position to defend their presence in the collection.

The obverse problem may be more difficult—that of the citizen who protests the absence of books which have not been selected. Such protests almost invariably come not from people who wish to read the books but from those who want them in the library for other people to read. They want the library to serve their propagandistic purposes. Suggested here is possibly a new principle of book selection. All public librarians consider very carefully every request from a patron for the addition of a particular title when it is clear that the patron wants to read the book. When it seems unlikely that anyone else in the community will want to read the title in question, the book is borrowed from another library. There is no reason, however, either to buy the book or borrow it because an interested citizen wants it to be available for others to read. The principle applies not only to books in the field of religion but to all other areas in which the patron may have an ulterior motive, be it politics, his views on the fluoridation of water, or parental interest in his own deathless prose or poetry. It applies equally to books offered as gifts. The librarian who would not buy a volume presented with the author's compliments should feel under no compulsion to add it to his library's collection.

Politics. "The Myth of Library Impartiality," first so described by Berelson,[5] is here generally recognized as such. Libraries cannot supply an equal number of titles on both or all sides of every political issue. They must follow the pattern of book publication and cannot wait for a title to appear on the "other" side before making a purchase. It is necessary, however, that the authentic and important books on every political issue which meets the normal selection criteria be acquired as they are published. And certain landmark books need to be added regardless of those criteria. *The Communist Manifesto, Mein Kampf,* and the *Blue Book* of the John Birch Society are classic examples.

The ulterior motive principle is relevant here also, particularly during presidential campaign years. *A Texan Looks at Lyndon,* by J. Evetts Haley, is only one example of books which many public libraries were urged to add to their collections for the propagandistic purposes of the donors. Some libraries added them; some did not; some placed them in pamphlet files as being "ephemeral" material—not a bad hiding place. One librarian added them with a flourish of local newspaper publicity as to why he did so.[6] This may have been good public relations but seems clearly inconsistent with the ALA Statement on Labeling [see Appendix].

Books as News. It happens occasionally that a book which does not meet the normal selection criteria of a public library is added later when, for one reason or another, it becomes news. *Peyton Place* will serve as an example. Literary trash by almost anyone's standards, this book was rejected by many public libraries following the normal selection process. "But," as one librarian has said, "when a book sells seven million copies, it becomes news as a literary phenomenon, and

---

[5] Bernard Berelson, "The Myth of Library Impartiality," *Wilson Library Bulletin,* 13 (October 1938), 87-90.

[6] "Dayton Tests Selection Policy Against Election Campaign Books." *Library Journal,* 89 (December 1, 1964), 4765.

should be added so that readers in general can discover what the fuss is all about."

In another area, *Race and Reason,* by Carleton Putnam, was not bought by the Arlington (Virginia) County Public Library because it gave biased, inaccurate information on the alleged basic inferiority of Negroes. The book's supporters protested vehemently to the library, then placed a bill before the Virginia General Assembly requiring mandatory inclusion of the book on the Board of Education's approved list for public schools. Thus the title acquired news value, and it became important for libraries to have it so that interested citizens could form their own opinions about the controversy. The director of the Arlington County Public Library then added *Race and Reason* to the book collection. Neither *Peyton Place* nor *Race and Reason* acquired intrinsic value because of their topical interest. One remains trash and the other remains inaccurate, and now that they are no longer in the limelight, no librarian should feel any compulsion to add them in violation of normal selection criteria.

Closed Shelves and Locked Cases. A substantial number of librarians whose book selection policies are relatively unrestrictive limit the practice of intellectual freedom by restricting the circulation of certain titles and certain classes of books. To say the books are shown in the card catalog and are available at the desk on request still places a barrier between book and patron. Nearly 80 per cent of public library patrons do not come to the library to obtain a specific book;[7] hence the book which cannot be found by browsing through the open shelves is lost to the overwhelming majority of library patrons.

Many of the titles which are not freely available on the open shelves are precisely the ones which ought to be there to be found and read by the patron who has no one to ask or consult for the needed information and who is too timid to allow a librarian to become aware of his need. Once the selection decision has been made to add a title to a library collection, that title should find its rightful place on the open shelves of the library.

Such closed shelf collections are justified in the minds of many li-

---

[7] Mary Lee Bundy, "Metropolitan Public Library Use," *Wilson Library Bulletin,* 41 (May 1967), 956.

brarians by a real or alleged need for the library to protect the books from theft or mutilation. The need may well be real for some books, including those which must be segregated for reasons other than their possible controversiality.

Segregation to protect the book, however, is probably overemphasized. To have several copies of a ten-dollar book stolen in a single year is a painful experience for library personnel and involves both budgetary and processing costs; a librarian's natural response is to find a way of putting a stop to it—such as placing all such books on closed shelves. The fact of the matter is that we have no evidence that titles with an alleged high theft potential are stolen at a greater rate than the average volume in the collection. It just seems that way. Some loss by theft is part of the cost of doing business on an open shelf basis and should be budgeted for in the same manner as losses by depreciation and obsolescence. Good unrestrictive selection policies developed in the cause of intellectual freedom should not be vitiated by restrictive administrative practices.

Age of Reader. Closed shelves are sometimes considered necessary as a means of keeping children and young people from finding books considered suitable only for adults. Other administrative practices are used to the same end under the presumption that some books are harmful to the young or in an effort to avoid controversy with parents who might think so. Indeed, the protest of only one patron about a book on the open shelves has served as a jail sentence for many books in many libraries. Librarians generally resist the withdrawal or destruction of a book, but too many do not hesitate to place it under lock and key.

Beginning on June 27, 1967, when the American Library Association Council unanimously approved a revised Library Bill of Rights as "basic policies which should govern the services of all libraries," any restriction on the use of the library by reason of the reader's age clearly became contrary to ALA policy. Paragraph 5 of the Library Bill of Rights now reads: "The rights of an individual to the use of a library should not be denied or abridged because of his age, race, religion, national origins or social or political views."

The insertion of the word "age" was a direct result of the 1967 Preconference Institute on Intellectual Freedom and the Teenager, sponsored by the Intellectual Freedom Committee, the American Association of School Librarians, and the Young Adult Services Division. Beginning with a brilliant address by Edgar Z. Friedenberg, then Professor of Sociology on the Davis campus of the University of California, speaker after speaker brought authority to bear on the fact that no evidence exists of a correlation between the reading of allegedly obscene materials and juvenile delinquency, and that, in fact, the typical juvenile delinquent reads hardly anything at all. A summary by Intellectual Freedom Committee chairman Ervin J. Gaines of the conference papers, which have not yet been published, may be found in the September 1967 issue of the *Newsletter on Intellectual Freedom*. In brief, the young person who is ready for the content of a book is also ready to handle that content; if he is not ready he will either not be interested in the book or will not understand and will pass over the portions his elders are concerned about on his behalf.

The librarian who would restrict the availability of books to young people because of actual or suspected parental objection to certain books being freely available to young people on the open shelves needs to bear in mind that he is not *in loco parentis* in his position as librarian. The job of the public and school librarian is to select books for a particular clientele in accordance with established policy. Not all books can be suitable for all members of a clientele, but all must be there for the use of those who can and want to read them. The parent who would rather his child did not read certain books or certain categories of books should advise the child, not the librarian.

Health and Medicine. Librarians are from time to time charged with censorship for not adding to their collections in the field of health, nutrition, and medicine books not regarded by the medical profession as authentic and reliable. *Dianetics*, by L. Ronald Hubbard, for example, was not added to the collections of the Brooklyn Public Library on the basis of a negative review in the *Journal of the American Medical Association*. More recently the Madison, Wisconsin, Public Library came under criticism for not stocking the books on nutrition written by Adele Davis. In a letter dated October 4, 1966, Assistant Director Orrilla Blackshear responded as follows:

When a person comes to the public library to obtain books

on nutrition or on health, he has a right to expect that the books he receives will fall within the broad area of accepted nutritional and medical practice. Anyone using the library to obtain technical information has the right to assume that the library will furnish such information from authoritative sources. In technical matters, we must depend upon authorities in the field for evaluation.

This problem was also touched on by Broderick, who noted that some librarians responding to her questionnaire about problem nonfiction were caught in a dilemma in connection with books in the field of nutrition.[8] One librarian who considered Taller's *Calories Don't Count* to be dangerous said the reserve list was too heavy for the library to withdraw the book. On the other hand, six libraries holding the book withdrew it from circulation when the United States Government instituted action against it.[9] Both situations point up a failure to think through the principles involved and reveal a lack of confidence in the librarian's own book selection judgment. Certainly a book which is dangerous should not be circulated by a library no matter how long the reserve list. Nor, when a library has decided a book is a desirable addition to the collection, should it be withdrawn just because a legal action has been instituted against it. Let librarians not be guilty of equating accusation with a formal determination of guilt by a court of competent jurisdiction.

In General. Other subject areas which librarians consider sensitive could be adduced, but enough examples have been presented to work toward some generalizations in behalf of complete intellectual freedom in the book selection process by the wholly intellectually honest librarian. A few words more need to be said in criticism of efforts by school administrators and public librarians to rationalize a restrictive attitude or position.

The pressure toward censorship in school libraries has sometimes

---

[8] Broderick, "Problem Nonfiction," 3373-8.

[9] Dr. Herman Taller was found guilty by a federal jury in New York City on twelve counts of mail fraud, one count of conspiracy, and violation of the Food, Drug and Cosmetics Law. See "Calories Author Guilty," *Publishers' Weekly* (May 22, 1967), 40.

been alleviated or eliminated by a compromise: the reading of the book in question is permitted rather than required. This serves to remove the impasse between the parent who objects to a particular book and his child who feels he must read it because it is in his school assignment. Thus a strong parental protest against one of four books on a required reading list in a Philadelphia high school was resolved amicably by the addition of three to the list and the requirement that any four of the seven be read. In Oceanside, California, when parents representing nine families requested that their children be kept out of the school library because of the presence of the *Dictionary of American Slang,* the request was denied; but school authorities agreed that the *Dictionary* would not be made available to these children, in accordance with general district policy to deny children access to books their own parents deemed objectionable. This practice seems to remove or to alleviate pressure, but it does not solve the problem concerning those materials which librarians or teachers believe every student should have access to or should be required to read. Were the principle to be generally extended to permit adjustment of curriculum and library resources for each individual child according to the predilections of his parents, public education soon would be a mockery and the school library an administrative shambles. School authorities and librarians must realize that there is no easy way to escape around the pressures toward censorship. Inevitably, sooner or later, they must be met head-on with a forthright defense of the principle of the freedom to read along with a very sincere and dedicated effort to educate the public concerned in the importance of the principle and the value of the books to which a vocal minority objects.

The public librarian frequently states that his reason for not buying a particular book is "lack of funds." The reason is used almost indiscriminately for books the librarian considers of dubious worth, those potentially a subject of controversy, and those so obviously superior as to be very expensive. Art books are a usual example. While most readers allow themselves to be put off by this specious answer, the reader who chooses to argue can almost invariably place the librarian in an untenable position. If the book in question is of dubious value the reader can find a host of volumes already on the shelves equally if not more dubious.

It is the same with the potentially controversial book. Any good collection already contains many books which have been involved in controversy and a good many more which may be.

Even in the case of the expensive art book, the librarian who says he cannot afford it because there are other needs that take precedence at a particular time is saying only that he considers those other needs to be more important to his community than the art book. There can hardly be a library so poor that it could not purchase a one-hundred-dollar art book if the selector considered that book to be more important to the community than the twenty or thirty other books the same one hundred dollars could buy. The plea of poverty is one which librarians must learn to avoid as being too easy an answer to an important question and one which only the casual inquirer will accept and which the intelligent reader considers either evasive or dishonest.

Another frequently stated reason for not purchasing a book is that there is no demand for it. The joker in the sentence is the absent modifier *known*. Some books are so obviously important or potentially of such great value that they must be purchased even if there is no known demand. Futhermore, since most books borrowed from the public library are found on the shelf by borrowers who did not know of their existence upon entering the library, the librarian has the obligation to provide the good and important books of our time so that his clientele may have the opportunity of finding them while browsing. Thus the argument of demand, or lack of demand, is equally specious. It causes the librarian to say or imply that no one in his community has the wit or the will to read the book in question—a stand no librarian can afford to take.

The librarian who understands Asheim's distinction between selection and censorship, who is wholly serious and conscientious in the process of selection need have no fear of a censor's success in a legal determination of an issue by a competent court. This position was admirably set forth by Edward de Grazia at the Washington Conference on Intellectual Freedom:

> It is my opinion that under present law no book selected by a librarian for his shelves can constitutionally be found obscene. Why? Because any such book must have at least some slight

redeeming social importance. The very act of library selection
testifies to and engrafts such importance upon it.

This is why, for example, the Kinsey Institute was able to
vindicate in court its constitutional right to import even so-
called hard-core pornography. The process of selection, the
institutional interest, can lend even otherwise "worthless" material the kind of importance necessary to activate the constitutional guarantees of free expression. Therefore, I believe
that libraries must have something like total immunity from
prosecution or external coercion in the exercise of their vital
functions.

The basic principle for librarians might best be described thus:
Any material selected by a librarian, in the exercise of his
function as a librarian, is protected. The protection extends
both to his acquisition and retention of the material, and also
precludes any valid prosecution of the librarian for acquiring
or retaining it. [10]

---

[10] Edward de Grazia, "Defending the Freedom to Read in the Courts,"
ALA Bulletin, 59 (June 1965), 507-15.

2

WRITING A
SELECTION POLICY

Although it is undoubtedly true that most public and school libraries have not prepared a written book selection policy, the fact that they ought to have written one can hardly have escaped the attention of their librarians. Documentation of this statement is abundant, and we need here refer only to Standard No. 87 in *Public Library Service,* [1] which reads as follows: "Every library should have a written statement of policy, covering the selection and maintenance of its collection of books and of nonbook materials."

For school libraries, the Board of Directors of the American Association of School Librarians have approved a statement of policy including this sentence:

It is believed that such a policy should be formally adopted by each school district as a basis for consistent excellence in choice of materials and as a document that can be presented to

---

[1] American Library Association, *Public Library Service* (Chicago: The Association, 1956).

parents and other citizens for their further understanding of the purposes and standards of selection of school library materials. [2]

Similar statements abound in the literature of the profession and in the official pronouncements of national, state, and local public and school library associations. The articulate members of the profession are unanimous in their support of the need for preparing a formal selection policy for every library, no matter how large or how small it may be. That more than a few libraries have not taken action may be laid to natural human procrastination rather than to disagreement or opposition, though some disagreement may indeed exist.

There are two major reasons for writing a book selection policy. The first, which may be said to have provided much greater impetus to librarians, is the importance of having a document in hand when a selection decision is challenged. Such policy statements have proved their value time and time again in minimizing both the possibility and the extent of the disturbance which a serious question about the presence or absence of a particular book might otherwise have caused. The very existence of the statement as evidence of the fact that a library staff has a selection policy which has been approved by the proper governing authority is likely to take the wind out of the sails of the would-be censor or propagandist.

The second reason for writing a book selection policy seems to be of equal importance and of much greater day-to-day usefulness, although it is infrequently cited by librarians and still less frequently utilized. This reason is simply the practical need to define the full scope of the selection activity in the library. Some definition is, of course, in the mind of every librarian as one book is chosen and another is not; otherwise he would be too undecided to act; but selection will be better and decisions can be made more consistently if a written selection policy guides the selector.

Most library selection policies are brief documents addressed too largely to the first objective only, that is, self-defense, and providing very little guidance to the library staff in the day-to-day selection pro-

---

[2] American Association of School Librarians, *Policies and Procedures for Selection of School Library Materials* (Chicago: The Association, 1961).

cess. A few are long enough to provide some guidance but only a handful are in sufficient detail to be really useful. It is possible that two documents are needed: first, a general statement of policy for the information of the public and for use in controversy; and second, a more detailed internal document for the day-to-day guidance of the library staff. The two could be bound together for some purposes and used separately for others.

The writing of a selection policy, if it is done seriously and deliberately, should produce other benefits besides the end product of a useful and workable policy statement. Among these is the intellectual stimulation afforded the staff in the process of thinking through an *a priori* statement of precisely what is to be in the library. Another is the public relations value of drawing the whole community into observing and participating in the process. The individual or organization which has participated in drafting the policy statement for the public library is much more likely to defend that statement and the library in any controversy that may arise and is much more likely to understand the entire scope of the library collection and its possible uses. In most communities the public has no conception at all of how books get into the library nor of the magnitude of the problems involved in selecting a maximum number of desirable titles from the wealth of material published each year, much of which has no place in any given library, not because it is bad, but because it is beyond the library's scope.

The actual writing of the policy statement should start with a meeting of the professional staff to discuss the need for writing a statement, the benefits to be gained from the process, and the anticipated usefulness of the statement once it has been written. The meeting should continue with some discussion of the technique to be used in the writing and particularly the need for making positive statements about the kinds of materials which are to be selected for the library, avoiding insofar as possible all statements negative or restrictive in character. It must be kept in mind that the concern is with a selection policy, not a rejection policy. Instructions on technique should include the concept of depth as well as breadth, so that the library staff would concern itself with the relative superficiality or exhaustiveness of selection in each literary form and subject area.

A division of the various subject areas among the professional staff would follow. The smaller the staff, the larger the areas would have to be; in very large libraries there might even be committees of the staff to work in each area. If possible these allocations, as well as the responsibility for selection itself, should take into account the subject background and interests of the staff members insofar as they are known. Some areas would need to be arbitrarily allocated; but such allocations can be considered a challenge rather than a disadvantage to the librarian who has not hitherto considered himself a specialist in typewriting or chess or eighteenth century poetry.

After some weeks, there might be a series of staff meetings to discuss and to edit the whole developing statement so that it meets with the approval and assent of the entire staff. A good deal of give-and-take discussion might occur during these meetings, as various members of the staff with varying intensities of exposure to the needs of the community argue both the extent and the depth to which the library ought to be selecting materials in various subject areas and literary forms. Remembering that the tone of the statement is to be positive rather than restrictive, a consensus should be possible in all cases; staff unanimity on the ultimate statement is not only desirable but attainable.

When there is general staff agreement that the best book selection policy possible for the time has been created, the librarian might well present a draft to the library board, the city manager, the city council, or other supervisory authority. Again the object would be to promote discussion, suggestions, possible revisions, additions, or better phrasing. These suggestions, all of which should be cordially and sincerely received, would then go back to another series of staff meetings for more discussion until the staff and supervisory authority are in substantial agreement.

If a properly positive attitude is maintained, disagreement is hardly expected. If a member of the board of trustees or the city council considers that the library ought to have a substantial collection in the field of public health for the use of the city health department, the library staff can have little reason for disagreement, at least in advance of the creation of such a collection. Conversely, if the library staff is firmly of the opinion that books in the field of medicine do not need to be collected in depth because of the excellent collection maintained by the county medical society across the street, no member of the city council is likely to disagree.

While this creative process is going on and the suggestions from the higher authority are being incorporated into the policy statement, the librarian or another qualified member of the staff ought to be presenting the draft of the policy statement to a wide variety of civic groups and organizations, such as service clubs, the PTA, the Garden Club, the Chess Club, and any other organization willing to schedule a librarian for a thirty- or forty-minute talk. The librarian would take along copies of the draft for distribution and would talk for fifteen or twenty minutes along lines somewhat like this:

> We at the library are writing a selection policy for your public library, and we need your help. We want this selection policy to be as broad and as representative of the needs of this community as it can possibly be. Here is a draft of what the staff of the library has written up to now. We want your opinions, your suggestions, your ideas of what you think ought to be in your public library. The library staff, through its daily contact with the members of your organization using the library, has a pretty good idea of what you need and want; these needs have already been incorporated into the policy statement before you; but because it is possible that some areas in which you are interested may have been overlooked, we would like to have your help in filling any gaps inadvertently left by the library staff.

In this talk the librarian might go over a few points to show the kinds of materials the statement is concerned with and conclude by asking for suggestions from the meeting; if there is no time he might request that suggestions be made later, orally or in writing, for careful consideration by the staff for inclusion in the policy statement. It may be anticipated that few good suggestions will be offered. But even if not very many usable suggestions are received in the course of a series of meetings that might extend over a year's time, the effort can still be considered to be worthwhile for getting community participation in the writing of the selection policy. The suggestions considered by the library staff and its supervisory authority to be useful and important are incorporated into the statement of policy, which then can be said to be substantially the work of practically everybody in town, at least everybody who is represented by one or more of the groups.

To gain the help, support, and participation of those patrons of the library who are not members of local organizations, the librarian should make copies of the draft policy statement available at various points of service throughout the library, along with a cordial invitation to examine the draft and to make suggestions to the librarian or any member of the staff. Again, probably few new and usable suggestions will be received. Nevertheless, it can reasonably be assumed that virtually all the patrons of the library have the opportunity to participate in drafting the library's selection policy. Even those who have made no suggestions will be aware of the fact that they have had the opportunity.

The policy statement should incorporate all usable suggestions from individuals and community organizations. After it has been completed to the satisfaction of the library staff and approved by the supervisory authority, it should be published as a separate document for internal use by the library staff, for use by patrons as the occasion arises, and for general distribution to interested individuals and organizations within the community. It would be desirable also to publish the whole document or substantial portions of it in the local press along with a complete list of the organizations which have participated in preparing the document. Before the use of the completed policy is discussed, it should be noted that the job, done once, is not likely to have been done for all time. Communities and their reading interests and needs change with the passage of time, as does the pattern of book production. Revisions of the basic policy statement will have to be made as conditions change, and the whole document ought to be reviewed at regular intervals, probably every five years.

The completed book selection policy, particularly if it has been prepared in considerable detail, can now be used by the library staff as a daily guide in the selection of materials for the library. With a firm statement in hand of the kinds of materials that belong in the library and, as a corollary, the kinds of materials that do not belong, the library staff will be able to do a more intelligent and more efficient job of selecting books for the library. The policy statement will be no substitute for knowing the collection or for knowing the clientele and the daily demands upon the collection, but it will be a useful guideline for deciding whether the next item in the current *Publishers' Weekly* should be passed over as being beyond the library's scope or should be considered seriously for inclusion in the collection. With such a guide the library collection over the years should become intrinsically better and in greater accord with the demands and needs of the library's clientele. As those demands and needs change, the policy will need to be changed as well; but if all such changes become the subject of staff discussion, there will be much less danger that selection will be done capriciously or in response to a temporary fad.

The occurrence of questions raised by staff or clientele about the reasons why certain books are in the library or certain other books are not there will be less frequent than daily selection decisions. The library selector may even raise the question himself incredulously: "Now why on earth did I ever buy that?" When such questions do arise, the book selection policy statement will provide a guide or a standard against which to consider whether the book in question is in line with the policy. If it is, and in nearly all cases it will be, the book selection policy statement provides a ready means to assist in explaining to the questioner why the book he is concerned about belongs in the library or does not belong there. The very fact that the library can show that it has a selection policy and that books are not bought capriciously or at the whim of a particular librarian, goes far to mollify the anxious or exasperated reader. Furthermore, when the policy statement is placed in his hands, the burden is placed upon him to show how and why the book in question was purchased, or not purchased, in violation of the policy.

In all such discussions in the privacy of the librarian's office and in the absence of public controversy, the librarian must be careful to retain his perspective and realize that selection errors can be made. If upon reexamination of the book in the light of policy, an honest judgment is made that the book does not belong and that a mistake has been made in buying it, the librarian must be prepared to admit his mistake and withdraw the book. A decision on such a question becomes a point of no return. If upon reexamination the book's presence in the collection is substantiated as being in line with policy, the librarian is bound to reaffirm the earlier decision. Should the case then become a matter of public controversy, the librarian prepares to stand behind the book and the library's statement of policy. Back of him in that stance the librarian will find the library board and the city council, for they approved the policy under which the book was selected. Only a little farther back will be all the individuals and organizations in town who participated in the formulation of the policy and who are now moved to back up the librarian who can show that the book in question belongs in (or does not belong in) the library in accordance with a certain paragraph of the official policy statement.

CHAPTER *3*

SAMPLE
SELECTION POLICIES

A considerable sense of misgiving accompanies this presentation of composite selection policies for public libraries, for the provision of a crutch may not be a good idea. The use of the word *model* is deliberately avoided because there is no such thing as a model selection policy which can be used in selection and defense by every library, by many libraries, or even by a few.

Even if it were possible to draft such a model policy, no librarian would be well advised to use it, either in selection or in controversy. To suggest that each library staff must learn by doing somehow misses the point, for learning to write a selection policy is not the objective. The selection policy is intended as a tool to enable a library staff to provide a good library collection, tailor-made to the needs, interests, and dreams of the community the library serves. It should be well balanced, yes; but balanced in the sense of a mobile rather than a teeter-totter. Specifications for making a teeter-totter undoubtedly exist, but who ever heard of specifications for a mobile?

To shift the metaphor, the day of the Carnegie library has passed, and it is no longer possible to dot the countryside with predesigned library buildings. It is neither desirable or possible to stock either the Carnegie or more modern buildings with identical collections. Not only must the collection suit the community it serves, but its development is necessarily conditioned by the staff which writes and uses its selection policy and defends the resulting collection.

To use the policy effectively in the selection process and to defend the collection successfully, the staff must have had the experience of thinking through and writing the policy statement. Still, crutches are sometimes useful even to the healthy and capable, and a few guidelines drawn from extant policy statements may be helpful in suggesting desirable coverage and scope, so long as it is understood that this stricture against copying is based on a more important concept than copyright.

The following statement is a composite derived from a large number of existing public library policy statements. Pertinent paragraphs have been borrowed verbatim or with only a minimum of editing to remove the more local references. All of them are keyed to the list of sources at the end of the chapter.

The statement does not cover more specific areas mainly because they were not mentioned in the policies examined; in addition emphasis here is on matters touching on intellectual freedom. Statements concerning forms of material, such as periodicals or documents, have been omitted. To achieve a maximally useful local policy, paragraphs should be written for a large number of other areas, so that guidance is provided to assist the librarian's selection in home economics as well as in sex, in poetry as well as in fiction, in engineering as well as in medicine.

I. ADULT BOOK SELECTION POLICY

The purpose of this book selection policy is to guide librarians and to inform the public about the principles upon which selections are made.

A policy cannot replace the judgment of librarians, but stating goals and indicating boundaries will assist them in choosing from a vast array of available materials.

Final responsibility for book selection lies with the librarian. However, the librarian will delegate to staff members authority to interpret and guide the application of the policy in making day-to-day selections. Unusual problems will be referred to the librarian for resolution. [1]

To further these general objectives, the library in its selection policies emphasizes its educational and informational functions. A book has educational value if it contributes to the positive growth of a person, either as an individual or as a member of society, whether that society be a peer group, the family, or the world. Including books that widen horizons, stimulate imagination and reflection, and enlarge experience, this definition enters into fields that a narrower one might classify as recreation or as aesthetic appreciation. The library's book selection reflects the importance of basic books of permanent value and books on current issues and problems.

The library recognizes its obligation to provide reference and research materials for the direct answering of specific questions and for continuing research. However, because of the availability of some highly specialized collections in the immediate vicinity intended primarily for exhaustive research . . . the . . . library weighs carefully its purchasing of very specialized works in certain fields. This does not mean that little or nothing is bought in these areas. Good working collections including standard works, classics, and popular titles are acquired in all needed fields. [6]

Selection is considered a judgmental and interpretive process, involving: a general knowledge of the subject and its important literature; a familiarity with the materials in the collection; an awareness of the bibliographies of the subject; and a recognition of the needs of the community. Along with a critical examination of the current production, continual consideration is given to book reviews, authoritative discussions of the literature of the subject, pertinent bibliographical publications, publishers' advertising media, and requests of library patrons. [3]

The library does not promulgate particular beliefs or views, nor is the selection of any given book equivalent to endorsement of the viewpoint of the author expressed therein. Within the framework of the

Library Bill of Rights and the Freedom to Read Statement [see Appendix] adopted by the American Library Association, it does provide materials representing all approaches to public issues of a controversial nature. The library is aware that one or more persons may take issue with the selection of any specific item, and welcomes any expression of opinion by patrons, but does not undertake the task of pleasing all patrons by the elimination of items purchased after due deliberation under guidance of the policies expressed herein. To provide a resource where the free individual can examine many points of view and make his own decisions is one of the essential purposes of the library. [5]

Use of the Library's Books

The library recognizes that many books are controversial and that any given item may offend some patrons. Selections will not be made on the basis of any anticipated approval or disapproval, but solely on the merits of the work in relation to the building of the collections and to serving the interests of readers.

Library materials will not be marked or identified to show approval or disapproval of the contents, and no cataloged book or other item will be sequestered, except for the express purpose of protecting it from injury or theft.

The use of rare and scholarly items of great value may be controlled to the extent required to preserve them from harm, but no further.

Responsibility for the reading of children rests with their parents and legal guardians. Selection will not be inhibited by the possibility that books may inadvertently come into the possession of children.

General Guidelines for Selection

1. The library takes cognizance of the purposes and resources of other libraries in the community and shall not needlessly duplicate functions and materials.
2. The library does not attempt to acquire textbooks or other curriculum-related materials except as such materials also serve the general public.

3. Because the library serves a public embracing a wide range of ages, educational background, and reading skills it will always seek to select materials of varying complexity.

4. In selecting books for the collections, the library will pay due regard to the special, commercial, industrial, cultural and civic enterprises of the community. [1]

Terms of Reference

Book selection may be described in terms of three dimensions: (a) DEPTH (b) RANGE or BREADTH (c) DUPLICATION

DEPTH is considered to be the comparative degree of concentration which the library will employ in a specified subject. Five terms have been adopted:

1. *Exhaustive*—Obtain or try to obtain everything available on the subject, within budgetary limitations.
2. *Comprehensive*—Select all materials available, excluding those items of doubtful value.
3. *Representative*—A well-rounded collection covering all phases of the subject.
4. *Selective*—Only the important basic, fundamental, or significant items; or those having current value or timely interest.
5. *Minimal*—Only materials of general information: such as dictionaries, encyclopedias, surveys.

RANGE or BREADTH is more difficult to define, inasmuch as it may be expressed in one case in geographic or national terms; in another case in subject terms; in another, in terms of a person or a group of people, or a period of time. Simply considered, range is the term used to characterize the outer limits of the collection policy for the specific subject.

DUPLICATION means simply the number of copies usually stocked of titles in the subject unit.

Stock will be maintained to differing degrees of saturation, as to particular books or subjects. Basic, landmark books, that are in perennial use, and that have stood the test of time, are to be stocked to a point where the normal demand can be met adequately. Shelf adequacy is the key to saturation rather than shelf-list adequacy.[3]

ART

The library attempts to acquire major books in art, architecture, sculpture and the applied arts, including standard works on the great periods, on influences and on men who have contributed to our cultural heritage. In the case of expensive books, a check is made with the local art institute, which has a good art library for reference use only.

Special consideration is given to books for the amateur artist and the art lover. Books about the home—its decoration, planning, landscaping, and furniture—are also emphasized. Books on the crafts and techniques of art to answer specific reference questions and to make identification for collectors are added.

Books of cartoons are bought only when they have historical or social significance as comment on the times, or as examples of the work of outstanding cartoonists. [11]

BIOGRAPHY

Biography includes autobiography, personal narratives and journals, diaries, and letters. All types are purchased, in varying quantity, including standard editions of classical works. Special attention is given to lives of pioneers and local personalities. Since the biographer must be eclectic in his use of material, biographical writing follows no prescribed rules or pattern. Documentation, or sound evidence, is looked for in relation to the nature of treatment, popular accounts being in a measure exempt from the rigid standards imposed on serious or academic studies.[2]

CHEMISTRY

"The literature of chemistry is like a great, inspiring mountain with a core of rich ore. It is inspiring because the work of great men, of many interested investigators is recorded there." Because of the excellence of the indexes and abstracts covering this vast amount of literature, it is the most accessible and usable area of all scientific endeavor. This fact of accessibility is one of the most potent factors in creating a demand for the literature and a need for supplying this demand.

A. The objective of selection in the field of chemistry and chemical processing is to develop a research collection of literature that has the widest possible breadth, width, and depth, so that the research chemist can come to the library with a reasonable expectation of finding the specific reference or piece of information he seeks. Since the larger proportion of his searching will involve the periodical literature, this form of material will probably take on a greater importance than in any other subject field.

The field of chemistry and chemical processing industries is related to most of the other physical sciences and the biological sciences, so that any limitations on these fields would indirectly limit it. For example: Biochemistry, health and medicine, engineering materials and their analysis, mining, geology, mineralogy, biology and physics all have aspects that are of a distinctly chemical nature.

B. Books in the field of pure chemistry and its subdivisions should be selected for readers of limited background and training as well as the highly trained research chemist. While the fundamentals of the subject are well established, there are varying points of view and theories in even these "basic books," so it is important that all are represented. The range of treatment of the subject should run from introductory textbooks to comprehensive treatises, and from general elementary books to extended treatment in specialized volumes. [3]

CIVIL SERVICE
An extensive collection of civil service study material is maintained and the best of this material is duplicated, within reason, to take care of the demand when examinations for initial entry or promotion are given. [11]

COMMUNISM
The library has authentic, well documented material on the Communist party in the U. S. and other parts of the world. It is the library's position that information concerning the methods, the nature and the extent of Communist actions and activity is essential for all citizens. In keeping with the Library Bill of Rights [see Appendix] the library does not prohibit material solely because of the political affiliations of the author. [10]

DRUGS

The library recognizes its responsibility to provide detailed and authoritative information on dangerous drugs. The library purchases materials which describe the history, chemistry, physiological and psychological effects, and the dangers of narcotics and other drugs, the treatment of addiction, and the social aspects of the problems. Generally, writings by addicts which delineate the sensations of dangerous drugs, case studies by specialists describing their work, dosage, and methods of administering are not purchased because they are outside the scope of the library's collection.[6]

ECONOMICS

The study of economics is both theoretical and practical. Besides books on theory and the various schools of economic thought, the library endeavors to provide a broad range of materials dealing with labor problems, money and banking, investment, public finance, real estate practice, and business literature closely related to finance and management in the technical book classifications. Works on economic subjects of a classical nature are well represented in the library's holdings, including the writings of contemporary economists.[2]

EDUCATION

Fairly heavy duplication is made of material on various phases of education, such as theory and philosophy, comparative forms of instruction, vocational and adult education, remedial reading, vocational rehabilitation, and the use of audiovisual material. The library also supplies standard works on the history of education, professional teaching methods, educational psychology, and school organization and administration on elementary and secondary levels, in addition to books on college life and the more formal aspects of higher education. College and university directories and curriculum catalogs are obtained for reference use.[2]

FICTION

Involved in the problem of selecting fiction is the existence of a variety of types of novels and the need to satisfy readers of differing tastes, interests, purposes, and reading levels. The library's collection, therefore, includes representative novels of the past and present, notable for literary quality and cultural value; historical and regional novels; character studies, biographical and psychological novels; novels relating to the fields of art, industry, science, social problems, and the professions; satire, fantasy, and humor; mystery and suspense, science fiction, western, and other adventure stories; romances; and short stories.

The library recognizes the importance of the novel as an educational tool, as a medium for recording and molding public opinion, and as an instrument for changing individual attitudes. The sound treatment of significant social and personal problems or of racial and religious questions through novels of wide reader appeal contributes much to the betterment of human relations. For this reason, a substantial number of novels of serious purpose are purchased. Due attention is paid to maintaining a basic collection in attractive editions of standard novels, the classics, and the semiclassics of world literature. Attention is given also to acquiring fiction useful in meeting the educational and recreational needs of an adult public of limited reading ability.

In selecting fiction the library has set up no arbitrary single standard of literary quality. An attempt is made to satisfy a public varying greatly in education, interests, taste, and reading skill. Under these circumstances fiction selection does not mean choosing only the most distinguished novels but also the most competent, pleasing, and successful books in all important categories of fiction writing. Staff members, when reviewing new books, consider a title in comparison with a good work which has been done in the writer's specific field. Naturally the literary criteria applied in the case of an experimental novel, for example, will differ from those by which a detective story is chosen.

However, it is the experimental novel rather than fiction written purely for entertainment that usually poses problems in book selection. The novel is a vigorous literary form, subject to change and innovation by writers to suit their differing aims. The author's purpose and his success in achieving it are the best guides in judging a novel at a time when ideas about structure and style are so varied and conflicting. In the past, plot and characterization have been considered essential to the novel, but in recent years plot has been almost abandoned by many leading novelists. The major interests among writers of serious fiction today are character and ideas, although plot may be said to survive in the development which takes place in the leading character in the course of the story. Readers, however, do not always look with favor on experimentalism, and the library's staff is aware that a novel distinguished for characterization and style must also possess a well-constructed plot, in order to be sure of a favorable reception among large numbers of readers. Titles that combine these qualities are sought and duplicated heavily, although care is taken to include representative works of experimental novelists and examples of new trends. [6]

FINE ARTS

Books on the fine arts cover an exceedingly wide range, from primitive beginnings to modern trends and developments in all countries. They take in music, photography, landscape gardening, sports and recreation, antiques and jewelry, dancing and the dramatic arts, and radio, television and motion picture production. Art itself is multiple and includes drawing, design, painting, sculpture, architecture, religious art and symbolism, ceramics, prints, and commercial art. Written and edited chiefly by critics, teachers, and connoisseurs, art books comprise museum guides, annuals and directories, dictionaries, encyclopedias, general and national histories, essays and biographical studies, handbooks, formal texts and manuals of instruction. Books in the field of music include biographical and reference works, histories of music, opera plots, orchestral, sacred and popular music, and descriptive accounts of musical instruments. [2]

FOREIGN LANGUAGE BOOKS

Use of the library's collection in a foreign language is a determining factor in acquisition. The titles added in each language are roughly proportioned to the relative size of the nationality group locally, the potential use of the collection and the availability of material in the language. Although the foreign-born population is comparatively small, the library in the last decade has experienced an increasing demand for books in foreign languages. Requests for these materials come chiefly from two groups of readers: the foreign-born, and a large number of students, teachers, and multilingual adults who read one or more foreign languages for pleasure or in connection with their professions or studies.

The responsibility for selecting material is distributed among the subject department heads. In selecting titles in all foreign languages, an attempt is made to buy representative fiction, biography, drama, etc., including the classics; standard and familiar authors of the past; the best of the modern writers; books describing cultural and religious traditions; and some books on current scientific, social, and economic problems.

In addition, a fair proportion of translations of standard English and American writers, particularly in the fields of fiction and biography, is chosen to acquaint foreign readers with American life and customs. Histories of the United States and texts or general descriptive works on American government in each foreign language, as well as materials on everyday problems of getting along in a new country are added. Children's titles in foreign languages may be included in adult collections if deemed useful, after consultation with the Coordinator of Work with Children. [6]

GENEALOGY

Selection is made on the basis of accuracy, objectivity, and clearness of presentation. The emphasis is upon the acquisition of printed records and vital statistics rather than published family genealogies. In the latter case, selection is made on the basis of inclusion of local or state individuals or families, extensive coverage of large or established families, and recommended titles as given in standard bibliographic sources. Emphasis is also given to the acquisition of materials which give information as to the how and why of genealogical work, i.e., information as to genealogical procedures, sources, publishers.[3]

GEOGRAPHY AND TRAVEL

In the field of geography the library purchases textual materials and atlases largely for subject coverage. Atlases are selected for their cartographic excellence and informational value in the areas of historical, economic, physical and descriptive geography, usually for reference purposes. Travel constitutes a major field in book selection, due to the popularity of the subject, stemming from the great increase in world travel in recent years. Books by well-known travelers and world authorities are purchased, including the personal experiences of explorers, scientists, and missionaries, as well as classic accounts and standard travel guides. [2]

GEOLOGY

Book material selected will be for the general reader. The collection will be limited to North American geology with complete coverage of state geology. The library receives some publications in the field of geology from other states. These will be continued and other states added as they will serve a need in the local area. Some of the state publications will be purchased as monographs.[3]

HISTORY

The library selects books covering all phases of human history, from the earliest times to the present, with emphasis on American history, the state, the region, and the county. Local histories are also sought out, especially of cities and areas of the county served by the library. Important printed source materials and basic bibliographies are acquired and preserved.

Relatively large numbers of the best available materials in historical fields are purchased, including both popular and scholarly works, in addition to classics and philosophies of history by professional historians and observers. These include books representing widely held or significant views and interpretations of historical events, selected without particular regard to literary style or formal scholarship. Highly specialized works, if purchased at all, are usually acquired in single copies. Essentially factual material is supplied liberally in the form of yearbooks and almanacs, encyclopedias, epitomes, and occasional textbooks selected for their informational or educational importance.[2]

LANGUAGE

Books on the subject of language include those dealing with linguistics, etymology and lexicography, in addition to readers and simplified classics for adults learning English and those studying foreign languages. Formal grammars are bought sparingly. Wordbooks of special type are also bought in few numbers, although dictionaries, including English, foreign, and "two-way" manuals, are bought freely for reference use. Spanish, French and German readers are purchased liberally, that is, the more reliable general texts containing both grammar and readings. Textbooks on unusual languages, such as Asiatic or American Indian dialects, are usually acquired as single copies, in relation to demand.[2]

LAW

The major consideration in the library's policy in the selection of law materials is the availability of the extensive county law library to all members of the legal profession and the obvious difficulties involved in the use of technical law materials by untrained laymen. The library provides a basic collection of standard and popular books for the general reader on such subjects as jurisprudence, history of law, court procedure, development of legal institutions, etc., with major emphasis on practices in the United States. Standard texts on special phases of the law are not purchased. Some textbooks on business law, used by high school and college students, as well as dictionaries, encyclopedias and phrase books are made available to a limited extent. The library does not attempt to provide books of court cases except a few standard collections of United States Supreme Court cases for the use of students.[11]

LIBRARY SCIENCE

The library science collection is intended for the use of staff members and interested members of the public. No attempt is made to assemble a complete history of libraries and library methods for research purposes.[11]

LITERATURE

The library endeavors to stock all American and English literary classics in the best available editions, important and popular contemporary titles, and representative works in English of other national cultures, ancient and modern. Selections are also made of anthologies, works of literary criticism and histories of general and national literature.[2]

LOCAL HISTORY

The library acknowledges a particular interest in local and state history; therefore, it will seek to acquire all state and municipal public documents, and it will take a broad view of works by and about the state's authors as well as general works relating to the state, whether or not such materials meet the standards of selection in other respects.[1]

MATHEMATICS

There will be comprehensive coverage and duplication in the area of practical mathematics and the "refresher" type books for home study. Because mathematics is so closely allied with the applied sciences and in order to provide material for the industrial interests of the community, advanced mathematics materials will be purchased. The publications from the principal mathematical societies will be obtained. Due to the wide interest and application of automatic digital computers among industries there will be extensive coverage of this subject both in books and periodicals.[3]

MEDICINE

The library recognizes its responsibility to supply authoritative, up-to-date, understandable material on health, hygiene, and common diseases. Medical and health books are selected with special care. Book selection in this area is influenced by the presence of several outstanding medical collections located in the city. . . . In view of increasing demands from the lay public for advanced materials, the library has amplified its original selection patterns and now buys more extensively than before in medical subjects. Many adults are entering the health-related occupations, and many already in them are studying for promotion. The medical and psychiatric social workers, the public health people taking advanced courses, the teacher studying special education, all are requiring materials of considerable coverage and depth. In an effort to meet these important needs the library buys extensively in the areas of psychiatry, mental retardation, alcoholism, narcotics, public health and sanitation, chronic diseases, and other medical-social problems, but avoids clinical case histories that justifiably belong in a professional medical library.

Books are purchased on several levels of difficulty: that of the junior and senior high school student, the college student, the adult layman, the medical and psychiatric social workers, the nurse (practical, student, and graduate), the teacher, and the public health worker. Material useful to the layman is sought in such subjects as psychiatry, geriatrics, obstetrics, environmental medicine, drugs, cancer, heart and high blood pressure conditions, the common chronic diseases, the addictions, and therapeutic diets. The library also buys for general readers and students a representative number of texts in such basic sciences as microbiology, anatomy and physiology, physiological chemistry, endocrinology, pharmacology, and more extensively, in the fields of food, nutrition, and nursing.

Clinical texts on diagnosis and treatment are not usually bought, but a few of the briefer texts on each of the main branches of medicine most in demand are provided in the reference collection. Persons needing technical and professional materials beyond the scope of this collection may consult medical libraries.[6]

MUSIC

The library buys books of musical history, theory, composition, and biography. It buys musical scores for which there is a specific demand, such as music representative of certain periods, and also has a small gift collection of part scores. Books of instruction are purchased only for the most commonly studied instruments, such as piano and violin.[8]

PHILOSOPHY

Philosophy may be said to comprise man's ideas about the nature of the universe and the meaning of life, the kind of being he is, and his relation to the world at large. Principal subdivisions within these broad fields of thought are metaphysics (theory of knowledge and being), logic (science of reasoning), aesthetics (theory of beauty), and ethics (study of moral conduct). The library buys the best books on all these related subjects, also important histories of philosophy and guides to philosophical systems. Textbooks and academic treatises by reputable authors are usually purchased in limited quantity. Classical works, both ancient and modern, as well as "self-help" books and popular histories of philosophy are those most often duplicated.[2]

PHYSICS

This area has developed into an "exact science" which is the basis of many of the other science fields. Because of its many ramifications it is important that this area have comprehensive coverage not only for the general reader, but for the technical research worker as well. Therefore publications of the societies will be purchased and the majority of the periodicals indexed in Section A of *Science Abstracts*. Due to the great importance of atomic physics there will be "saturation" selection in those materials which are written for the layman.[3]

POLITICAL SCIENCE

Political science is the study of the theory and organization of government, political parties, comparative forms of government, and international relations. Closely related is public administration, or the management of local, state, and Federal executive branches of government, including military science and services, a composite subject of considerable current interest. In addition to supplying standard works, the library encourages the selection and use of books showing the origins of our institutions and ways to further development in democratic living.[2]

PRINTING AND PUBLISHING

Buy widely because of local interest in printing. Books which are of use to the student or to the businessman in explaining the fundamentals of the printing processes will be purchased in triplicate or to the number of five in the case of an exceptionally fine manual. Histories of printing when offering a fresh and more interesting approach both in subject treatment and format are purchased. Type specimen books are bought when they offer new material or appear to be good replacements for older, worn-out copies. Very specialized books in typesetting are not bought. Books on publishing and bookselling are selected widely, but unless the book concerns a local or nationally known publisher one copy is sufficient.[3]

PSEUDOSCIENTIFIC BOOKS

The library buys representative titles expressing views which may not be generally accepted but for which there is public demand. Such titles may be in the fields of extrasensory perception, health, and unidentified flying objects. The library buys representative titles on subjects not generally accepted by the scientific community. Such titles may be in the fields of palmistry, graphology, and spiritualism.[7]

PSYCHOLOGY

Psychology may be defined as the systematic knowledge and investigation of the phenomena of consciousness and behavior. Books for the public on mental hygiene and child and adult psychology are chosen principally for their value in the home or as general texts for educational purposes. Standard works on the theory and practice of educational psychology, animal and human intelligence, personality and aptitude tests and related subjects may be selected for purchase in limited numbers as aids to teachers and researchers. Books of advice on the problems of everyday living, written in popular style, may be selected for wider distribution.

Although representative works reflecting trends in important schools of psychological thought may be bought for special use, no attempt is made to cover advanced fields primarily of interest to the medical profession. This includes textbooks on clinical psychology, psychotherapy and psychoanalysis, in addition to studies in abnormal behavior, therapeutic hypnosis and psychological testing.

In the field of pseudopsychology, particularly occultism, the library purchases with extreme caution, since much of the data, from a scientific standpoint, is of an unverifiable nature. Debatable subjects include astrology, fortune-telling and palmistry, numerology, sorcery, spiritualism, hypnotism, and telepathy. Serious studies investigating mental or spiritual phenomena, as in parapsychology (including extra-sensory perception and psychic research), may be purchased in limited quantity for reference purposes.[2]

RELIGION

Because religion is a subject of such deep and intense concern to so many people, it is important that the library, as a city public library and a statewide resource center, maintain a balanced and fairly extensive collection.

Standard works relating to the world's major religions, such as the Bible, the Talmud and Midrash, the works of Luther and Calvin, the Koran, the Mahabharata, are provided in so far as they are available in the original and in other languages of interest to readers. . . . Important versions of the Bible and other religious texts and scriptures are purchased as well as editions important for their literary or artistic value or for usefulness of format (such as annotated "reference" or large print editions). Costly reprints and other ornamental editions of religious classics are added only when they have unusual artistic or bibliographic interest.

The most authoritative and useful of the various reference works (e.g., encyclopedias, commentaries, histories) which introduce, explain, and interpret the scriptures and religious classics are selected, with care being taken that works written from the various major religious points of view are represented where they are available and pertinent. The history of religion and the histories of various faiths and communions, theology, the beliefs and practices of the religions of the world, comparative religion, mythology, atheism and agnosticism, and the psychology and philosophy of religion are represented by authoritative works, with emphasis on those which are of interest to the educated layman.

Lives of Christ and biblical characters, lives of saints, church fathers, and other religious biographies, practical books on worship, liturgy, and ritual, church management, the ministry, sacraments, religious education, missions, pastoral work, sermons, spiritual life, personal religions, and moral theology; stories of hymns and hymnals, collections of prayers, books of devotion and meditation, and books of inspiration are added when they meet the criteria of clear and effective presentation and factual accuracy (where pertinent). Since users of the library vary widely in educational background and reading ability, an effort is made to choose well-written materials to fit differing needs.

The library recognizes an obligation to provide information about major religious denominations represented locally. For such denominations it provides official publications such as books of discipline, service books, up-to-date directories, and periodicals. Information on small sects and those that have few adherents ... [among the library's patrons] can usually be provided by official statements of doctrine, pamphlet material, and directories.[6]

SEX

It is a responsibility of the library to provide an adequate supply of information on sex, designed for all age levels of readers not trained in medicine or related disciplines. Books and materials purchased are those which are authoritative and scientifically sound in treatment. Books for varying levels of educational and differing social and religious customs are provided.

On the subject of sex deviations, the library attempts to keep a stock of carefully selected materials including studies, reports, and some personal accounts. Highly specialized, clinical, technical works do not come within the scope of the library's collection.[6]

SOCIAL SCIENCES

The collection represents the major social, political and economic trends. Less publicized movements, especially of local origin, are not overlooked since the library is often the only place where such information is preserved. The library specializes in several subject areas where an effort is made to build up strong historical and current collections. Some of these are: social theory, slavery and race problems, foreign relations, economic theory, labor relations, investments, real estate, insurance, accounting, advertising, business methods, market research, constitutional history, world government, criminal cases and crimes, woman suffrage, history of transportation, and local material.

Conservative, liberal, revolutionary, and reactionary schools of thought are represented. Care is exercised to represent all sides of controversial questions and to maintain balance in the collection. Because of the nature of the community and the size of the collection, books presenting extremes of opinion which would not be suitable in a smaller collection can be added. Books containing points of view which may be offensive to certain people are purchased if representative of an important segment of opinion, as in certain areas of the race problem. Publications which are purely propaganda are acquired if they contain official documents or speeches of important public figures.[12]

SOCIOLOGY

A vast field of inquiry and analysis, sociology includes social psychology, urban and rural sociology, population, social organization and change, community planning, family relationship and counseling. The library selects widely in this area from among general surveys and special materials of interest to researchers and social workers, as well as popular books on marriage, social etiquette, and family life on both adult and young adult levels.[2]

II. YOUNG ADULT BOOK SELECTION POLICY

It is the aim of service to young adults to help them through books to find self-realization, to live in their communities as citizens of this democracy, and to be at home in the world. This aim is constantly kept in mind when books are selected for the young adult collections. The book selection policies for young adult work are based on the following principles:

1. The young adult collections should be composed of books that widen the boundaries of the adolescent's thinking, that enrich his life, and help him fulfill his recreational and emotional needs. Materials to help him prepare his school assignments are in the reference and general adult collections rather than the young adult collections. However, school demands are considered if the books requested are both of a recreational nature and in the field of special interest to teen-agers, such as World War I, popular science, plays.

2. While our aims are clearly stated, the rules for selection cannot be written out ahead of time except in general terms, for each book must be considered separately. In other words, books have both faults and virtues, and if the virtues far overbalance a fault, a book may be included. With this in mind, the so-called "touchy" areas in book selection for teen-agers are handled as follows: (a) The use of profanity or of frankness in dealing with sex may be controversial, but when a book opens a clearer vision of life, develops understanding of other people, or breaks down intolerance, these virtues must be weighed against the possible harm to be done by some shocking word or passage in the book, particularly where taste rather than morals is offended. (b) Books of sex information for teen-agers belong on the open shelves of young adult collections. It is important that young adults gain sound information on this subject. If the books are treated as are interesting books on other subjects, much can be done to give teen-agers a healthful attitude toward sex. (c) Religious books of an obviously denominational nature whose primary purpose is to present one sect as superior to another are not purchased for young adult collections, nor are books that belittle any faith. Only well-written books that make no attempt to sway the emotions of the adolescent toward or against any one faith should be included in special collections for young adults.

3. All types of readers must be considered in setting up a book collection. Simple teen-age stories of boy-girl relationships teach young and reluctant readers a love of reading—the first step in the development of any reader. At the other end of the scale is the older, better reader,

often the superior student, who is forming his own philosophy and wishes to read adult titles that throw a clear light on the process of living.[6]

III. CHILDREN'S BOOK SELECTION POLICY
The Children's Department has long taken to heart Paul Hazard's words, as he spoke of "an American innovation: the libraries reserved for children," where all respect is shown the child. He is not asked if he is rich or poor, Catholic, Presbyterian or Quaker. He has complete freedom. From the hundreds or thousands of books within reach of his hand, he takes one that pleases him. He may remain ten minutes or several hours. . . ."

The Department's primary aim is to serve the whole child—his recreational, informational and inspirational book needs—and those who serve him, parents, teachers, organization and church youth workers, authors and artists in the children's field. Books are purchased for a wide range of ages and abilities and interests. Specifically, children are served by the Children's Department book collection from infancy through eighth grade. Retarded as well as advanced readers are considered in the selection.

Promoting the love of reading "for reading's sake," developing appreciation and discrimination, satisfying natural curiosity, contributing to the growth of the child as an individual and a future citizen of responsibility in an expanded world—these are also goals. In other words, books are purchased with the idea that the young reader is not only the influential adult of tomorrow, but a "person" in his own right today.[9]

Selection for Specific Age Levels
PRESCHOOL
In the Children's Department and many of the branches separate collections entitled "Parents' Collection" are maintained. These collections contain books for use with infants and preschool children, as well as titles on the care and training of children from the adult collection. The juvenile titles are a selection of books of jingles, rhymes, poetry, simple animal and folk literature, ABC books, handicraft books

for kindergarten age, and the childhood classics, such as Brooke, *Johnny Crow's Garden;* Gág, *Millions of Cats;* and Lenski, *The Little Train.*

ELEMENTARY SCHOOL

Children's books are sought which will keep pace with the wide range of children's interests in the elementary grades. In some fields books have not kept pace with the child's widened horizons at the grade or reading level needed. The library considers it a responsibility to provide books on all subjects of major interest to children and at a reading level appropriate to the age of interest.

JUNIOR HIGH SCHOOL STUDENTS THROUGH THE EIGHTH GRADE

Service to children extends through the eighth grade of school. Recreational reading for these older readers consists chiefly of titles in the fiction, biography, and science fields. Easy reading materials with plot and subject matter, such as career, sport, mystery, adventure, and love stories (example: Breck, *Maggie*), are included.[6]

Specific Areas

FOLK AND FAIRY LITERATURE

In the belief that this type of book frequently forms the basis of a child's literary heritage in addition to advancing an understanding of the world's peoples, the library considers it a responsibility to include titles which will provide as complete coverage of this area of literature as possible. Each new title in this classification is evaluated against previous titles of the same type, as well as in relation to its place in filling in gaps in the folk literature of the world. An effort is made to include a variety of editions, particularly when the compiler, translator, or illustrator is of sufficient distinction to add to the stature of the book.[6]

HUMAN RELATIONS

The library considers the removal of prejudice and ignorance regarding racial or religious groups of people one of its major responsibilities, and to this end makes a continuous effort to include in its book collections for children titles which foster healthy attitudes along these lines. Books on all countries, races, nationalities, and religious groups are carefully selected; and those which bear any serious discriminatory remarks or attitudes are not purchased.[6]

RELIGION

The library considers the child's spiritual development the primary responsibility of his home and his church, but with the realization that the spiritual side of man is all important to himself and to his fellow creatures, supplies certain books on religious subjects for children. Bible stories, lives of the saints, and biographies of religious characters are bought when the particular title meets the required standards for children's books generally. Books on the customs and traditions of religious faiths are occasionally purchased, such as Fitch, *One God* and titles of general spiritual content as Jones, *Small Rain,* and Walpole, *A First Book about God;* but books or pamphlets of specific religious teaching or practice are not purchased.[6]

SEX

The library believes the *introduction* of the subject of sex to the child to be primarily the responsibility of the home. The library's responsibility is to provide books written in a simple, dignified, and scientific manner on the processes of human physical development and reproduction. . . .[6]

Sources

[1] Minneapolis Public Library, 1965.
[2] Los Angeles County Library, 1958.
[3] Milwaukee Public Library, 1959.
[4] Washington, D.C., Public Library, as quoted in *Public Libraries Division Reporter,* No. 4 (October 1955), 54.
[5] Mountain View, California, 1965.
[6] Enoch Pratt Free Library, 1968.
[7] Library Association of Portland, 1960.
[8] Kalamazoo Public Library, 1963.
[9] Dallas Public Library, 1961.
[10] Waukegan Public Library, 1962.
[11] Dayton and Montgomery County Public Library, 1966.
[12] Los Angeles Public Library, 1962.

CHAPTER 4

EVALUATING
THE POLICY

Challenges to the presence or absence of a particular book constitute a piecemeal and haphazard evaluation of the practice of book selection over a considerable period of time, whether or not that practice has been based on a well-developed written policy as described in Chapter 3. Evaluation of selection policy and practice should not be left to the censor's capricious whim. Evaluation should be as carefully planned as the policy itself to ensure a continuous revision of the policy on the one hand, and a serious check on the quality of the collection on the other. Both are important and both are apt to be neglected under pressure of more urgent matters in even the best of libraries. If professional time and care are expended on book selection in the development of a good collection, then effort must also be expended to make sure that the resulting collection is good *per se* and also well-suited to the needs of the library's actual and potential clientele.

The literature on the theory of collection evaluation is sparse almost to the point of nonexistence. Except for brief attention to the public library by Carnovsky,[1] and a more general pragmatic treatment by McDiarmid,[2] both now more than fifteen years old, and a recent descriptive essay by Williams,[3] no authority in the library field has addressed himself to an *a priori* philosophical consideration of how a library collection ought to be evaluated, what the criteria ought to be, or where the boundary lies between excellence and mediocrity.

Librarianship being the empirical science it is, this lack of theory has not inhibited the practice of collection evaluation, particularly manifest in the many surveys of public and academic libraries which have come into the literature during the last three decades. A large majority of these surveys, when their scope was at all general in character, have paid some attention to the book collection and have made value judgments on the basis of empirical findings. An account of some of the techniques used and the ways in which the results have been interpreted may prove useful to librarians who wish to embark on one-time or continuing studies of their collections. Such studies may well provide useful background knowledge and information to assist in resisting censorship, and should in all cases enhance the librarian's knowledge of his collection, on the basis of which daily decisions are made.

Gross size. It is almost a truism that the larger the library, the more apt it is to have good books or books people are most likely to want. If book selection is of indifferent quality, the library is also more apt to have inferior books, but this corollary has rarely been faced or admitted. Absolute size at one point in time, however, is in itself meaningless until it is compared to something else, such as the same library at some other time or other comparable libraries at the same time. Thus a collection twice as big as it was ten years ago may be said to be twice as good, or a library twice as large as another one with comparable clientele and objectives may be said to be twice as good.

Comparative evidence is frequently gathered by relating the gross size of a given public library to about ten libraries in other cities with

---

[1] Leon Carnovsky, "Measurement of Public Library Book Collections," *Library Trends*, 1 (April 1953), 462-470.
[2] Errett Weir McDiarmid, *The Library Survey* (Chicago: American Library Association, 1940), pp. 100-18.
[3] Edwin E. Williams, "Surveying Library Collections," in *Library Surveys*, edited by Maurice F. Tauber and Irlene R. Stephens (New York: Columbia University Press, 1967), pp. 23-45.

similar demographic characteristics. The library low or below average in total number of volumes may be adjudged to be inferior to the others on such a list. All such judgments are made on the assumption that libraries buy good and bad books in comparable proportions—a proposition which more refined criteria than gross size tend to disprove, but not to a significant extent.

The Checklist Method. More pertinent than a simple statement of gross size is the evaluation of a library collection through the use of a checklist of supposedly good books. A library holding a high proportion of the books on the list is considered to be a better library than one holding fewer. The assumption is generally acceptable provided that the checklist has not been previously used as a buying guide. The checklist method is a sampling procedure. Though particular books are sought in the library's collection, what really is being evaluated is the practice of book selection over the last x number of years. The assumption is that if y per cent of books on the list are in the library, then y per cent of all books represented by the scope of the list are also in the library. The assumption will never be proved, partly because of the impracticality of developing a list of *all* the books which ought to be in a library, and partly because agreement on such a list could never be achieved.

Many relatively standard bibliographies have been used as checklists in evaluating library collections; but the publications of The H. W. Wilson Company have been used most frequently, especially the *Public Library Catalog*, the *Senior High School Library Catalog*, and the *Children's Catalog*. Choosing a checklist is a fine exercise in determining validity, for which firm guidelines do not exist. It is necessary to be intellectually certain that the titles on the checklist do belong in the collection under study, or would have belonged at the time they were published. Evaluating a collection is a sampling procedure which also involves an evaluation of the whole selection procedure during the period covered by the checklist. Choosing the checklist embodies a judgment that the books it contains belong in the collection; using the checklist carries with it the assumption that all comparable books published during the same period also belong. The checklist should never be so long as to suggest that *only* the books on the list belong in the collection.

When the obviously applicable bibliography has been used as a buying guide, or an aspect of the collection is under examination for which no existing list is considered suitable, a special list is constructed for the purpose. Thus Leigh put together for the *Public Library Inquiry* a list of 126 titles made up of "the twelve fiction bestsellers, the twelve 'notable works' of the year's fiction as selected by an ALA committee of public librarians, twelve works of fiction selected by professional book critics as among the year's best in quality; also thirty each of (1) the year's nonfiction best sellers, (2) the librarians' list of 'notable' nonfiction, and (3) the critics' consensus of best books as compiled by us from book reviews." [4]

The details of the results of the checking process do not concern us here, but it might be noted in passing that the 58 libraries included in the sample held substantially more of the best sellers and "notable" books than they did of the "best" books chosen by the critics. Speculation at this juncture is irrelevant, but it can at least be noted that high scores on the lists of "notable" books could have been occasioned by the use of those lists as buying guides.

This conclusion was confirmed by a small student study conducted at the University of Oregon in the spring of 1967. Donald W. Ownby checked the lists of "notable" books for 1964, 1965, and 1966 with the catalogs of the Eugene and Springfield public libraries immediately after the list for 1966 had been published. Both libraries held a substantially greater number of the 1964 and 1965 lists, which could have been used as buying guides, than they did of the 1966 list, which had been published too recently to make such use possible.

Consensus of Expert Opinion. Although it has more frequently been used in evaluating college and university library collections, the practice of asking the presumed "experts," the users of the library, about the adequacy of the collection can be applied to public libraries also. Requests for individual titles not in the collection are of course carefully considered by the selecting authorities in all libraries, but library patrons cannot be said to be very vocal concerning their opinions on collection adequacy. They need to be asked. Questions have varied

[4] Robert D. Leigh, *The Public Library in the United States* (New York: Columbia University Press, 1950), pp. 77-8

from the general, "Is the collection in your field adequate for under-graduate study?" to the very specific, "What titles are needed to bring the collection in your field up to an acceptable standard?"

Results of a recent study of public library use in the Baltimore metropolitan area are revealing:

> When public library patrons go away unsatisfied, it is because they cannot obtain the materials they require and this is either because the books they want are out or because the library does not have them at all. Of those unsatisfied persons who gave their reasons: 47.0 per cent wanted a book or books which were out; 35.9 per cent wanted a book not in the library; 14.4 per cent could not locate material on the necessary subject; 6.4 per cent found that material was outdated; 6.1 per cent thought the material they found was on too elementary a level; 2.0 per cent located material that was too advanced; and 12.9 per cent indicated various other reasons for their dissatis-faction.[5]

Assuming the original data are complete, here is a wealth of material for study and use by the book selectors of the area.

On-Shelf Status. However good the results are of evaluating a collection by checking a list with the card catalog, the practical effectiveness of a collection can be much lower if few or none of the books can be found on the shelf at a particular time. The patron who wants help in taking color pictures at ten o'clock on a cloudy morning is not helped if *all* of the good books in the collection are out in circulation, are at the bindery, or were published in 1910. On-the-shelf status of holdings in many segments of the collection must be evaluated in addition to, or instead of, in-the-catalog status. While the library concept does imply successive use of the same volumes, care must be taken that no patron in search of subject material goes away empty-handed. A good book on color photography should be available to every person who comes in at ten o'clock on a cloudy morning.

Bookstock, Circulation, Additions. Though a formula can never

---

[5] Mary Lee Bundy, "Metropolitan Public Library Use," *Wilson Library Bulletin,* 41 (May 1967), 956-7.

be arbitrarily applied, there should usually be some justifiable relationship between library holdings in various subject areas, annual circulation in each area, and the number of volumes added to each area every year. Statistics ought to be developed from time to time to enable the librarian to consider this relationship for each major subject and form division of the collection in an effort to discover whether certain changes in emphasis might not be in order. Two opposite examples of possible results of such an analysis should suffice to illustrate the point:

Let us say that the collection in philosophy amounts to 2 per cent of total nonfiction holdings, and circulation during a given year is found to be 0.5 per cent of the nonfiction circulation. If it should then be discovered that 6 per cent of the nonfiction added during the year is for the philosophy collection, a question arises which needs consideration. The existing collection may be large but poor and thus does not circulate. It may be in need of augmentation. Substantial weeding may be in order. Book production in philosophy may have been unusually rich. The philosophy collection may be located in a dark corner on the bottom shelf, and it may be in need of promotion; or the librarian may have allowed his own keen interest in philosophy to influence unduly his selection policy and practice.

Conversely, it might be discovered that the collection in home economics represents 4 per cent of nonfiction holdings and 8 per cent of annual circulation. When it is discovered that annual accessions amount to only 2.5 per cent of the total, a similar question needs consideration. With 4 per cent of the collection doing 8 per cent of the work, why has the collection rated only 2.5 per cent of the additions? Were all of the good new books added? Is more duplication in order? Is the average loan period shorter? Or does the philosopher-librarian have a low opinion of the importance of domestic economy?

There will be other questions in other fields and certain special considerations in all fields. A large reference collection may show no circulation at all. In most libraries the size of the collection in history will almost certainly be disproportionate to either circulation or additions. The circulation of the small collection on unidentified flying objects may be out of all proportion either to its importance or to the number of titles available in print. The importance of the evaluation procedure lies in providing the librarian with comparative information on the emphases normal day-to-day selection activities bring to the library's collections, in enabling him to evaluate those emphases field by field, and in making such changes of emphasis in selection as are shown to be warranted.

Evidence of Use. Once books are in a library, another criterion of book selection has been added: their use. Although many modern charging systems do not create a record of use as a by-product, special procedures can be developed to serve a particular objective. While some books must be in every public library whether they are used or not, the number of such books is surprisingly small. After the Bible and Shakespeare, any three librarians might be able to agree on eight other titles, but the eleventh would occasion some discussion, and the one hundred and first possibly could not be agreed on at all.

Lists of basic book collections for public library branches contain fewer than 7,000 titles.[6] None of the lists of recommended books for public libraries contain more than 11,000 titles. None of the prefatory statements maintain that all of the titles should be in any library. The word "need" is frequently found, the phrase "in demand" less frequently. Always there is the consideration of whether the book will be used by the clientele of a given library. Librarians do not like buying books which, however intrinsically good, find no readers. Two of the more interesting studies of book use were conducted by the Racine, Wisconsin, and Evansville, Indiana, public libraries.

In Racine librarian Forrest Mills selected a work slip for every fifth nonfiction title purchased during 1955 and checked its circulation in December 1956 and again in December 1958. The original sample contained 347 items, reduced by loss to 322 by the time of the second check of circulation. Mr. Mills found that the average circulation per title was 7.11 and 13.2 at the two checkpoints, that the highest number of circulations per title was 37 in 1956 and 68 in 1958, and that the lowest circulation was zero. Careful study of the titles which had not circulated at all should provide considerable guidance to the selection activity of the Racine Public Library staff.

---

[6] There are about 6900 titles in *A Basic List of Adult Books for Branches of the D.C. Public Library* (Washington, D.C.: The Library, 1960).

In a study of the relative circulation of good and poor books in the Evansville Public Library, Goldhor concluded that:

> It would appear from the data available in this study that the best books are not necessarily the most widely read. If libraries buy good books and poor books in equal quantities, they will be read in approximately equal numbers. It is to the credit of this library that, in fact, it has more of the better books (and more copies of the better titles), and therefore in net balance more of the better books are borrowed. . . . But the conclusion of this study is that there is in fact a real basis for the value theory of book selection and that it is not likely that public library patrons will differentiate the better from the poorer books or read the former significantly more often than the latter.[6]

In Summary: The selection process only begins when the book is selected; the process continues throughout the life of the book until it is ultimately discarded or relegated to storage. The selector is, as Carter and Bonk would have it, a builder of library collections; moreover he cannot escape his role as a maintainer of the collection for which he is responsible. When the book has been selected and ordered, the librarian needs to examine the book when it arrives (if indeed it had not been read prior to selection), keeping in mind such questions as: "Is this what I expected? If not, why not? How did I guess wrong? Whose judgment was at fault? Did the publisher misrepresent the book? Was a review misleading?" Conscious answers to questions like these will not only assist the selector in making future selections, but will enhance his knowledge of the collection to the point where no potential censor can successfully challenge the place of a book in the collection.

The process of collection maintenance should continue through observation of each book's use and the use of the several hundred subcollections which make up a library's stock-in-trade, through noticing the need for mending and rebinding, and through making periodic evaluations of the adequacy of each subcollection in number of titles and

---

[6] Herbert Goldhor, "Are the Best Books the Most Read?," *Library Quarterly*, 29 (October 1959), 251-5.

in number of copies. Newly published bibliographies and lists of good books are routinely checked to test the efficacy of the book selection policy; the use of slowly moving titles is promoted and "dead" and obsolete titles are discarded or relegated to storage. Again, the objective is to know the collection so well that the book selection process is constantly being improved, the collection is being enhanced, and potential restrictive tendencies are minimized.

CHAPTER 5

THE ROLE OF
PROFESSIONAL ASSOCIATIONS
AND STATE LIBRARY AGENCIES

The contribution of the professional association at the national, state, and local level in the interest of intellectual freedom in libraries has not been small and should not be minimized. The best effort and much personal sacrifice of time and energy have gone into these endeavors by the leadership of the profession throughout the country in the various ways described in this and the next chapter. It must also be said, however, that these efforts have usually been general, educational, and hortatory. They have almost never consisted of specific, concrete assistance to a librarian, a teacher, or a book in trouble; where there have been specific overtures or actions, there is little evidence of their efficacy.

These statements are descriptive rather than critical of a situation which may very well have to be as it is. Tendencies toward censorship are local and have to be fought locally; neither side takes kindly, in general, to help—which is apt to be labeled interference—from outside experts. Thus, the major thrust of the profession has been to provide information, argument, and statements of policy in an effort to give the local librarian encouragement and support in time of need, and to persuade him to prepare for trouble during periods of relative calm. The present volume can accurately be described as just such an effort—something to make use of before the censor pounds the desk out front.

Something more may need doing in order to make qualified professional and legal help available to beleaguered librarians and booksellers, and the American Library Association, after long working toward the creation of such an office, succeeded in establishing one on December 1, 1967. The effort was not successful earlier, presumably for budgetary and administrative reasons. The cause of the problem may be rather in the essentially local matter of the librarians' confrontations with the tendencies toward censorship. Librarians do not need lawyers or even legal-defense funds so much as they need interested, intelligent, and alert local citizens to speak up when the issue is joined. They would do well to identify and organize such support well before the issue arises, and such is the general drift of the activities described below. The new ALA Office for Intellectual Freedom, under the direction of Mrs. Judith F. Krug, is budgeted to perform an information, supportive, and referral service; legal assistance is not yet within its charge, but the Association in the fall of 1969 was moving toward the creation of a support fund to assist librarians who lose their jobs in the defense of intellectual freedom.

The Committee on Intellectual Freedom of the American Library Association was created in May 1940, with the long, carefully restrictive title, Committee on Intellectual Freedom to Safeguard the Rights of Library Users to Freedom of Inquiry. Its purpose was stated a year later as follows: "To recommend such steps as may be necessary to safeguard the rights of library users in accordance with the Bill of Rights of the United States and the Library's Bill of Rights [see Appendix] as adopted by the Council." [1]

The essentially advisory nature of this charge remains very much the same today. The most recent revision, voted by the Executive Board on January 29, 1951, reads as follows:

> VOTED, That the powers of the ALA Committee on Intellectual Freedom and the Board on Personnel Administration

---

[1] *ALA Bulletin,* 35 (September 1941), 34.

in the areas related to the Loyalty Resolution and the Library Bill of Rights be limited to observing, investigating, and calling attention to the pertinent policy statement and to protesting as a board or committee any actions which appear to violate the policy statements if so authorized by the President and Executive Secretary; that where more delegated action is required the board or committee be charged with making a recommendation to the Executive Board for action; where the Executive Board disagrees on a correspondence vote, the matter must be held over until the next meeting of the Executive Board.[2]

The Committee remains powerless to act on its own. Virtually all activity must be authorized by the President and the Executive Secretary, and any desired action must be recommended to the Executive Board, which does the acting. It would be difficult to imagine an arrangement more stultifying to effective committee discussion or more inimical to effective action in so important an area of ALA and professional life. Assuming it wanted to, the Committee could never act fast enough to be of any assistance in a local situation. Until this defect is remedied, until the Executive Board is willing to give the Committee on Intellectual Freedom its own intellectual freedom, no librarian can expect his professional association to give concrete support to his defense of the Library Bill of Rights. Until such time, the Intellectual Freedom Office at ALA Headquarters cannot hope to reach its full effectiveness.

Approximately fifty state and local library associations have formed committees on intellectual freedom. These have varied greatly in amount of activity and relative effectiveness, depending in large part on the nature of the charge creating the committee, and on the interest and aggressiveness of the committee membership, particularly the chairman. The California committee has been notable for its vigorous and forthright action, particularly before legislative committees considering new restrictive legislation. Other state committees have

---

[2] American Library Association, *American Library Association Policies* (Chicago: The Association, 1961), p. 56.

published brief reports to the effect that no cases have been "called to their attention." The committee that waits for a call quite frequently has nothing to do.

Yet in theory the state and local committees should be in a much better position than a national committee to know what is happening and, knowing, in a superior position to act positively on that knowledge in the cause of intellectual freedom. Notwithstanding their relative ineffectiveness to date, the formation of state and local intellectual freedom committees deserves encouragement. Someone must have the responsibility for action if there is to be any action. At the state level the committee is probably best located within the state library association so that it may speak for as large and influential a body of librarians as possible.

Intellectual freedom committees at the local level have been neither prevalent nor consistently active, their tendency being to come to life or spring to action when a particular issue arises or the restrictive atmosphere becomes particularly oppressive. Their membership has rarely been limited to librarians, and leadership has often been non-librarian in character.

A notable example is the Long Island Intellectual Freedom Committee created by the Nassau-Suffolk School Library Association in 1964 which included representation from some fifteen other local and state organizations.[3] On the state level, the New Jersey Committee for the Right to Read, formed in 1964, has run up a notable record of achievement, including the publication of the best analysis of the relationship between the reading of pornography and overt behavior now extant.[4]

Other local groups include Audience, Unlimited, of Rochester, New York, formed in 1964, and the Illinois Freedom to Read Committee, organized in Chicago in 1967. Both are the result of police harassment of booksellers and were formed to fight illegal police activity in

---

[3] *American Library Association Newsletter on Intellectual Freedom,* 13 (November 1964), 74.

[4] New Jersey Committee for the Right to Read, *A Survey of New Jersey Psychiatrists and Psychologists Pertaining to the Proscription by Legislation of Sexually Oriented Publications for Persons Under 18 Years* (Caldwell: The Committee, 1967).

the courts and in the press. Librarians and booksellers have rarely joined forces in their fight against censorship, just as if intellectual freedom were divisible. But then, librarians have never been jailed and rarely come to the defense of works they do not stock.

One exception must be noted. When 21,000 copies of the April-May 1964 issue of *Evergreen Review* were seized by the county district attorney on the complaint of a bindery worker, the Nassau County Library Association's Intellectual Freedom Committee within four days filed a letter of protest with the district attorney with a copy to the press. The Committee also prepared an affidavit used by Grove Press in its successful court case challenging the seizure.

The library profession has not been alone in its concern with infringements of intellectual freedom and the right to read, but except for the American Civil Liberties Union, activity of other organizations has been broadly advisory and educational only. The ACLU has not only published important and far-reaching statements of policy, but its many local branches have often assumed leadership in fighting censorship cases in the courts. The index to the *Newsletter on Intellectual Freedom* for the period from 1952 through 1966 includes 123 references to the anticensorship activity of the ACLU and its affiliates, more than for any other organization except ALA itself.

In a major policy statement following a three-year review of the issue of censorship of allegedly obscene material, the ACLU on May 28, 1962, declared that "the constitutional guarantees of free speech apply to all expression." [5] Although urging acceptance of its no-censorship position in order to strengthen the protections of the First Amendment, the ACLU said it recognized that Federal and state antiobscenity laws do exist and are being invoked. When they are used, the ACLU stressed, the following standard should apply: "Any governmental restriction or punishment of any form of expression on the ground of obscenity must require proof beyond a reasonable doubt that such an expression would directly cause in a normal adult, behavior which has validly been made criminal by statute." [6] The ACLU pamphlet of guidance to local com-

---

[5] American Civil Liberties Union, *Obscenity and Censorship* (New York: The Union, 1963), p. 3.

[6] *Ibid*, p. 4.

munities entitled *Combatting Undemocratic Pressures on Schools and Libraries,* published in 1964, is the most positive and forthright statement extant on the need for and the techniques of opposing fringe pressure groups in our society.

The National Education Association's Commission on Professional Rights and Responsibilities has been actively interested in matters relating to intellectual freedom, as has the National Council of Teachers of English, but none of their activities have been as specifically supportive at the local level as have those of the ACLU. The NEA Commission's *State of the Nation Bulletin* No. 5 in January 1966 presented comparative statistics on various restrictive practices as surveyed in 1960, 1962, and 1965, and concluded they were increasing. The Commission also published a position paper in 1964 entitled *Freedom to Teach—Freedom to Learn.*

In 1962 the National Council of Teachers of English issued an excellent pamphlet entitled *The Student's Right to Read.* It included a useful suggested form, Citizen's Request for Reconsideration of a Book [see Appendix]. Its more recent *Obscenity, the Law and the English Teacher* (1966), containing two papers by John P. Frank and Robert F. Hogan, is more ambiguous in its impact. *Censorship and the Teacher,* by Kingsley Widmer, published by the American Federation of Teachers, is much more militantly for complete freedom on the part of teachers to choose curricular materials.

Although there is no basis for disputing Monypenny's statement that "state library executives have generally been in the front ranks of those opposing the critics of local libraries and of attempts to censor book circulation,"[7] that one sentence is virtually all he has to say about the matter. The 1963 *Standards for Library Functions at the State Level* have this to say in Standard no. 3: "The state through its state library agency should exercise leadership in maintaining freedom to read and freedom of access to materials of varying use within the state."[8] The paragraph which follows this statement speaks of resistance to the efforts of self-appointed censors and the invocation of legal machinery

---

[7] Philip Monypenny, *The Library Functions of the States* (Chicago: American Library Association, 1966), p. 24.
[8] American Association of State Libraries, *Standards for Library Functions at the State Level,* (Chicago: American Library Association, 1963), p. 7.

for dealing with subversive and pornographic literature. It also refers to the various views set forth in the Freedom to Read Statement and the Library Bill of Rights [see Appendix]. It is not a strong statement. Clearly, intellectual freedom has not been a major concern of the state library agencies, whose primary emphases have been developmental and budgetary. There is probably an inverse correlation at work here. The author has had more than one conversation with state library executives who were reluctant to oppose restrictive legislation in the same legislature considering a state-aid bill.

Though on the side of the angels in theory, state librarians have been no less restrictive or tolerant of restrictions in practice than have other librarians. Their activity in behalf of intellectual freedom has consisted largely of responding to correspondence from librarians or trustees in local difficulties, writing supportive letters to editors, and sponsoring occasional workshops (the one held in Wisconsin, which is described in Chapter 6, is a notable example). It must also be said that local librarians have not welcomed the intervention of their state librarians in their local confrontations with the tendencies toward censorship.

PROFESSIONAL ACTIVITY IN
BEHALF OF
INTELLECTUAL FREEDOM

The purpose of this chapter is to present in some detail, for the guidance of state and local intellectual freedom committees, a considerable array of devices and techniques, ranging from the very general policy statement, usually promulgated far in advance of any particular issue, to the very specific local action after an issue is joined. Emphasis cannot be placed too strongly or too frequently on the importance of developing general statements of policy and of organizing individual, group, and press support far in advance of the need for defending the integrity of a library collection. The rather natural use of military terminology is not without its pertinence. The librarian who has prepared a good offensive position in the cause of intellectual freedom, and has taken care to make that position known in the community, will not only be strategically situated to withstand an attack, but will rarely be confronted with an attack at all. A good offense is indeed the best defense.

Statements of Policy. The most important statement of policy is the one developed by each library staff for its own guidance in selecting books for the library's collection. The case for such a policy and a guide to writing it were presented in Chapter 2. A composite though incomplete policy statement derived from those of twelve public libraries comprises Chapter 3. This is not to be considered as a model to be copied. It is intended to be used merely as background reading by each library staff as it engages in the important and difficult intellectual task of writing a policy statement for the selection of materials for a particular library at a particular time. If the policy statement is written positively, with general and local inclinations toward censorship in mind, it will serve as a bulwark in the defense of intellectual freedom in addition to its other uses.

The early history of the Library Bill of Rights and other major American Library Association statements of policy has been recorded by Berninghausen,[1] to whom the reader is referred also for details concerning the ALA Intellectual Freedom Committee. The Committee did not come into being until a year after the Library Bill of Rights was adopted on June 19, 1939, at the first session of the San Francisco conference of the American Library Association, in a text which was to remain substantially unchanged until the 1967 San Francisco conference. An implied change was made by official action of the Council on February 3, 1951, to the effect that the Library Bill of Rights "shall be interpreted to apply to all materials and media of communication used or collected by libraries." On February 2, 1961, the ALA Council added paragraph 5, having to do with the right to library privileges without regard to race, religion, national origins or political views. The word "age" was added to the list in 1967, as was "social views."

The revised Library Bill of Rights as unanimously adopted by ALA Council in San Francisco on June 27, 1967, may be found in the Appendix as Document No. 1. In addition to the removal of certain dated phraseology, the new text represents a major change of emphasis from enlisting the aid of allied groups to pledging the cooperation of libraries with "all persons and groups concerned with resisting abridgment of free expression and free access to ideas."

---

[1] David K. Berninghausen, "The History of the ALA Intellectual Freedom Committee," *Wilson Library Bulletin*, 27 (June 1953), 813-17.

Other important statements of policy developed by the ALA Intellectual Freedom Committee include a Resolution on Loyalty Programs (1950), and Labeling Library Materials (1951). Their language is somewhat dated, but their import and impact are as sound and as useful as ever. They are reproduced in the Appendix as Documents No. 2 and No. 3, respectively.

Two other documents warrant special mention. One is the 1953 Freedom to Read Statement, Document No. 4 in the Appendix, notable because it was developed jointly by librarians and publishers and subsequently endorsed by three other national organizations. It is dated now, and the new version of the Library Bill of Rights moves the official Association position much further along, but it remains an important document, and for more than historical reasons.

From the lofty statement of principle in the Library Bill of Rights in 1939, it took the Association until 1962 to derive its statement How Libraries and Schools Can Resist Censorship. This detailed outline of steps to be taken both before and after a local tendency toward censorship becomes manifest, which appears as Document No. 6 in the Appendix, is, in a sense, a logical precursor of the present volume. Adopted by Council on February 1, 1962, the statement has been widely distributed both as a separate document and as a supplement to the September 1965 and November 1968 issues of the *Newsletter on Intellectual Freedom*. Librarians who are willing to stand on principle need weapons with which to fight, and this provides a good one.

Unlike the American Library Association, whose brief and limited charge to its Intellectual Freedom Committee is described in Chapter 5, some of the state associations have developed detailed statements of policy for their intellectual freedom committees. Outstandingly forthright in its delegation of full and immediate authority to act in behalf of the association is the policy developed in 1958 by the Intellectual Freedom Committee of the California Library Association and the Book Selection Policies Committee of the School Library Association of California and duly adopted by the executive boards of both associations on May 9, 1958 and March 18, 1958, respectively. Now more than ten years old, this statement of policy (Document No. 8 in the Appendix) may still serve as a model for other committees.

Information Kits. One of the more usual functions of intellectual freedom committees has been the gathering and dissemination of information about censorship and ways of combating it. One manifestation of this function is the intellectual freedom kit containing in a folder or envelope a variety of the kinds of documents assembled, for very much the same reasons, in the Appendix to this volume. The California Library Association has produced three such kits, the earliest in 1954. The Wisconsin Library Association and the Nassau-Suffolk Library Association in New York State have also made significant contributions in this area. Editions have never been large (usually under 500) and their selling prices have been nominal.

Newsletters. Materials in kits are loose and removable; from one point of view this is one of their virtues. One can find and place into the hands of an individual a document which may serve an immediate need, but it may also never get back into the kit. The search for a more permanent format has resulted in the publication of special issues of state library journals concerned with censorship and intellectual freedom. Significant efforts of this nature have been published in *Illinois Libraries* (May 1966), *The Bay State Librarian* (October 1966), *Pennsylvania Library Association Bulletin* (May 1963), and *Wisconsin Library Bulletin* (May-June 1964). So far as is known, however, no state or local library association has ever regularly published a journal devoted to censorship and intellectual freedom. The field has been left to the American Library Association, which began publication of its *Newsletter on Intellectual Freedom* in March, 1952.

Early issues were mimeographed. A printed masthead showing "Intellectual Freedom Committee of the American Library Association" as publisher was first used for Number 7 of Volume I, dated May 1953. Letterpress format was achieved in June 1960, when printing was undertaken by the Freedom of Information Center of the University of Missouri School of Journalism, an arrangement which lasted for two years. Size of issue has varied from four or five mimeographed pages to the sixteen printed pages almost standard in 1969. Frequency of publication was irregular in the early years, then it became quarterly, and ultimately bimonthly in 1963.

To date, the editors have been Paul Bixler (1952-1956), Leslie W.

Dunlap (1956-1957), Donald E. Strout (1957-1960), Everett T. Moore (1960-1961), Donald V. Black (1961-1962), and the present writer (1962-   ).

The editorial policy of the *Newsletter* was well stated by Everett T. Moore in the June 1960 issue:

> We will continue to call attention to situations and incidents that threaten the freedom to read. More particularly, our reporting of news and comment on events will be directed mainly to matters affecting library policies and librarians' freedom of action. We immediately disclaim any attempt to draw a line between the problems that face us as librarians and those that beset publishers and booksellers and educators. With these groups we must make a common front or ultimately face greater difficulties without the support we need. But although censorship is a common danger and must affect us all if it affects one of us, we are primarily concerned with the responsibility of the librarian to detect threats to his freedom and to build defenses against censorship.

Currently, the following kinds of material are included in the *Newsletter* as being pertinent to a general journal on intellectual freedom, published by the Intellectual Freedom Committee of the American Library Association. The texts of official statements by the ALA or its Intellectual Freedom Committee, including statements made before congressional committees and in *amici curiae* briefs filed in state or Federal courts, are usually printed in full. Similar official statements by regional, state, and local library associations and their intellectual freedom committees are recorded in full or in abstract. All incidents of censorship or alleged censorship of libraries are recorded, whether they originate outside the library or within it. The aim is to make the *Newsletter on Intellectual Freedom* a journal of record in matters of intellectual freedom relating to libraries, librarians, and their professional associations.

But as has been said before, intellectual freedom is not divisible, nor can reporting be limited to library matters only. Important infringements on academic freedom and restrictions on freedom of the press are reported as corollaries of the librarian's concern with intellectual freedom. Arrests for violations of local, state and Federal obscenity statutes are usually not recorded unless the title of a particular book, magazine or motion picture is reported; convictions and sentences are similarly reported only when the publications in question are identifiable. The object is to provide news and guidance about changes in the climate of legal opinion and judicial decision. Higher court decisions, especially those of the state courts and the United States Supreme Courts are reported in full because of their potential long-range effects.

Other content includes material reflecting important changes in the censorship climate abroad, well-written and potentially useful newspaper editorials, book reviews, bibliography of the current literature, and an occasional letter to the editor. The overall intent is to provide a record of library activity in the whole area of intellectual freedom and to place that record in the larger intellectual context of the society in which the library operates.

Through most of its history, the *Newsletter on Intellectual Freedom* has had the field to itself, not only in librarianship, but in the nation and in the world. All of its erstwhile contemporaries have been concerned with censorship in general, with only an incidental interest in library problems. One of these was an occasional, sometimes annual, sometimes more frequent, publication of the American Book Publishers Council initially called *Censorship Bulletin* and, later, *Freedom-to-Read-Bulletin*.[2] It was replaced, in effect, by a new monthly, *Freedom to Read Bulletin*,[3] published by the Bureau of Independent Publishers and Distributors. Lineal successor to all of these is the bimonthly *Censorship Today*, edited by Doris Fleishman, and published in Los Angeles since July 1968.

Two organs of local organizations formed to fight the encroachment of censorship are *The Readers' Right*,[4] published quarterly by the New Jersey Committee for the Right to Read, and *Audience Unlimited News*[5] of Rochester, New York.

This catalog would not be complete without mention of the *NODL*

---

[2] First issue, December 1955; last issue, Fall 1963.
[3] First issue, October 1966; last issue, December 1967.
[4] First issue, 1964; last issue, May 1968.
[5] First issue, March 1964.

Newsletter,[6] the monthly publication of the National Office for Decent Literature. Basically a list of paper books and magazines not approved for youth, the *NODL Newsletter* includes in the first issue of each quarter news of "progress" in restricting the distribution of "not approved" publications (including some "not approved" by other organizations). A similar attempt at reporting progress toward censorship is the *National Decency Reporter*,[7] official organ of Citizens for Decent Literature, Inc. of Cincinnati, Ohio. Except for important court decisions, the content of these two journals almost never overlaps that of the *Newsletter on Intellectual Freedom*. The serious student of encroaching censorship must read all three.

Workshops and Institutes. Developing viable statements of policy, assembling kits of information, and editing newsletters constitute important basic and fundamental activity on the part of relatively few people. To be effective they must be supplemented with promotional effort at professional meetings, institutes, and workshops to get amplification, interpretation, and practical detail into the minds and hearts of the working librarians whose job it is to implement policy at the local level. One of the earliest and most successful of such efforts was the Work Conference on Book Selection Policies at the 1955 Philadelphia conference of the American Library Association. Its report remains one of the basic landmark documents in this area.[8]

A decade later the American Library Association followed up with its Washington Conference on Intellectual Freedom, which resulted in an impressive array of papers providing inspiration and ammunition to the foes of censorship.[9] The Washington Conference was limited in scope to literature for adults, but repeated reference to and demand for a similar effort in the field of young people's literature resulted in the 1967 San Francisco Preconference on Intellectual Freedom for the Teen-ager. The papers have not been published, but a good summary by Intellectual Freedom Committee Chairman Ervin Gaines was pub-

---

[6] First issue, vol. I, no. 1, Summer 1956.
[7] First issue, vol. I, no. 1, March 1963.
[8] American Library Association, Committee on Intellectual Freedom, *Public Libraries Division Reporter*, 1 (October 1955), 1-65.
[9] American Library Association, Committee on Intellectual Freedom, *Freedom of Inquiry, Supporting the Library Bill of Rights* (Chicago: The Association, 1965). Also published in the *ALA Bulletin*, 59 (June 1965), 469-533.

lished in the *Newsletter on Intellectual Freedom* in September 1967. The Conference resulted in the insertion of the word "age" in paragraph five of the Library Bill of Rights [see Appendix], thus placing the American Library Association for the first time squarely against any censorship at all for anybody, no matter what his "age, race, religion, national origins or social or political views."

The state library associations have been active in this area also. The California Library Association cosponsored the Fiske report [10] and the ensuing Institute concerning it, which resulted in the significant collection of papers edited by Danton.[11] A useful example of how potentially or actually controversial books can be analyzed to further their acceptance is the discussion "Significant and Controversial Novels" presented by Mrs. Helen H. Lyman and Mrs. Orrilla Blackshear at an institute on the public library-school library relationship in Milwaukee in 1961.[12] Important also amid an atmosphere of restrictiveness involving *Tropic of Cancer* and *The Last Temptation of Christ* was the Preconference Meeting on Intellectual Freedom held by the California Library Association in November 1964.

Legislative Activity. Librarians as individuals and in organizations have the opportunity to participate in the legislative process at the national, state, and local level. The American Library Association has in recent years made formal presentations before congressional committees considering restrictive legislation in the areas of allegedly obscene and subversive materials. The most recent of these may be found in the official hearings and in the July 1967 issue of the *Newsletter on Intellectual Freedom.* Appearing before congressional committees is not usually possible for individuals, but letters to committees considering specific legislation are always welcome and weigh more heavily in committee deliberations than is commonly believed. Congressmen do need the help of knowledgeable professionals, and one cogent and rea-

---

[10] Marjorie Fiske, *Book Selection and Censorship* (Berkeley: University of California, 1959).

[11] J. Periam Danton, ed., *The Climate of Book Selection* (Berkeley: University of California, School of Librarianship, 1959).

[12] Wisconsin Free Library Commission, *Proceedings of the Eighth Institute on Public Library Management* (Madison: The Commission, 1961).

sonable argument well presented in a letter will effectively counter many more lengthy emotional harangues.

All of the foregoing is even more true at the state level where legislators are closer to their constituents and need and want guidance on the many abstruse and technical matters demanding their attention and their considered judgment. Comparatively few of the state intellectual freedom committees have been active in the state capitals, but committees in New Hampshire, New Jersey, New Mexico, Texas, and Wyoming have made important forays in recent years in behalf of intellectual freedom and have usually been successful. The California committee has a long and impressive history in the Sacramento legislative halls and has played an important role in defeating restrictive legislation in almost every biennium since 1955. That memorable year has been well described by Mosher in an essay setting forth in detail the battle fought to defeat legislation which would have hamstrung the selection policies of school libraries in California.[13] Another year the Book Selection Policies Committee of the School Library Association of California caused the introduction and passage of legislation to revise a paragraph in the Education Code which was being used by county auditors to refuse payment for books having the words "God" or "religion" in their titles.

State legislative committee hearings are open to any organization, lobbyist, or individual who wishes to speak on either side of every bill being heard. Often the librarian is the only speaker against a potentially restrictive measure; the difficulty of the role is matched only by its importance, and librarians need to learn how to play it well. This includes calling on and getting acquainted with committee members in advance to explain the librarian's point of view and to hear theirs, so that additional data and argument can be marshaled before the committee hearings.

Letters to the committee chairmen and to key members are of the utmost importance also. Consideration of each bill frequently begins with the report of a tally of letters received on either side. The position of the librarian testifying at the hearing is much strengthened if his col-

---

[13] Fredric J. Mosher, "Setting the Stage in California," in Danton, *Climate of Book Selection,* pp. 50-65.

leagues have previously expressed themselves in writing. Defeat in committee does not mean the end. Calls can still be made to key legislators now known to be favorable to the library position in order to enlist their support on the floor. After legislative action is complete, assuming a measure has been passed, there is still time to make the library position clear to the governor as to why he should or should not sign a particular bill into law.

Court Briefs. Generally speaking, the climate of intellectual freedom has been less restrictive in the courts than in the legislative and executive branches of national, state, and local governments. The growing understanding of the constitutional guarantees of freedom of expression contained in the First Amendment has led the higher courts to overturn much restrictive legislation and to reverse convictions obtained under it. In the higher courts it is usually possible to petition the courts to consider an *amicus curiae* brief setting forth the position of an interested organization or individual.

The American Library Association presented such a brief to the United States Supreme Court in the *Tropic of Cancer* case, which was ultimately decided in favor of the bookseller who had been convicted in Los Angeles and had lost his appeal in the California Supreme Court. The procedure is an important one, is not to be undertaken lightly, and is never without expense. It takes competent legal counsel who, even though willing to prepare a brief without compensation as his contribution to the cause of intellectual freedom, cannot be expected to bear the not inconsiderable expenses himself. Librarians and their associations must be prepared to underwrite such costs from time to time in last-ditch efforts to prevent new restrictions on the right to read and the freedom to select the books patrons need and should have.

The Local Scene. Important and necessary as all of this professional association activity on the national and state levels is, it must be remembered that most library confrontations with the encroaching censorship occur on the local level and are resolved there. The patron personally raising a question about a particular book can frequently go away with a greater understanding of the librarian's position after an hour's discussion of the book and the more general problem of providing a variety of reading for a wide and heterogeneous clientele. The protest received in the mail can be similarly answered, often to the apparent satisfaction of the patron. The use of a formal "Request for Reconsideration of a Book" form will either discourage the filing of a formal protest or will provide a firm and specific charge for consideration by the governing authority.

Such responses to criticism, frequently *pro forma,* will never necessarily be so; for librarians cannot adopt the position that they are above criticism or that their selections are always in accordance with library policy. Of course, the valid protest will be resolved by the librarian without recourse to a formal hearing. Any governing authority with confidence in its librarian will usually accept the librarian's stand. Even so, an atmosphere of serious and impartial consideration of each formal protest must be maintained. Not all the battles will be won, but it is significant that the defense against censorship which is presented vigorously and well is almost invariably successful. The initial protest is often consciously or subconsciously an effort at censorship by intimidation; when the librarian is firm in reasoned resistance, he may expect to avert most actual confrontations and to win those which do become public issues.

APPENDIX

BASIC DOCUMENTS

1.   Library Bill of Rights
        The Council of the American Library Association reaffirms its belief in the following basic policies which should govern the services of all libraries.

1. As a responsibility of library service, books and other library materials selected should be chosen for values of interest, information and enlightenment of all the people of the community. In no case should library materials be excluded because of the race or nationality or the social, political, or religious views of the authors.

2. Libraries should provide books and other materials presenting all points of view concerning the problems and issues of our times; no library materials should be proscribed or removed from libraries because of partisan or doctrinal disapproval.

3. Censorship should be challenged by libraries in the maintenance of their responsibility to provide public information and enlightenment.

4. Libraries should cooperate with all persons and groups concerned with resisting abridgment of free expression and free access to ideas.

5. The rights of an individual to the use of a library should not be denied or abridged because of his age, race, religion, national origins or social or political views.

6. As an institution of education for democratic living, the library should welcome the use of its meeting rooms for socially useful and cultural activities and discussion of current public questions. Such meeting places

should be available on equal terms to all groups in the community regardless of the beliefs and affiliations of their members, provided that the meetings be open to the public.

Adopted June 18, 1948.
Amended February 2, 1961, and June 27, 1967, by the ALA Council.

2.   Resolution on Loyalty Programs

WHEREAS, A democracy must preserve freedom of thought and expression if it is to survive; and

WHEREAS, Loyalty investigations of library employees may create an atmosphere of suspicion and fear and tend to limit intellectual freedom by rendering it hazardous to hold or express other than popular or orthodox views; and

WHEREAS, Librarians have a special responsibility to provide information on all sides of controversial issues, but cannot do so if intellectual conformity becomes a factor affecting their employment or tenure; and

WHEREAS, The American Library Association has received evidence that loyalty tests may easily lead to the violation of the constitutional rights of library employees, and in some cases already have done so; therefore, be it

Resolved, That we, the Council of American Library Association, strongly protest loyalty programs which inquire into a library employee's thoughts, reading matter, associates, or membership in organizations, unless a particular person's definite actions warrant such investigation. We approve the affirmation of allegiance to our Government. We condemn loyalty oaths and investigations which permit the discharge of an individual without a fair hearing. We hold that in a fair hearing the accused is furnished a statement of the charges against him, is allowed to see the evidence against him, is given an opportunity to prepare and to present his defense and to question his accusers with the aid of legal counsel, is presumed innocent until proved guilty, and is given the opportunity, if adjudged guilty, of judicial review.

Adopted July 21, 1950, by the ALA Council.

3.   Statement on Labeling

In view of our own convictions and those of other practicing librarians whose counsel we sought, the Committee on Intellectual Freedom recommends to the ALA Council the following policy with respect to labeling library materials:

Librarians should not use the technique of labeling as a means of predisposing readers against library materials for the following reasons:

1. Although totalitarian states find it easy and even proper, according to their ethics, to establish criteria for judging publications as "subversive," injustice and ignorance rather than justice and enlightenment result from such practices, and the American Library Association has a responsibility to take a stand against the establishment of such criteria in a democratic state.

2. Libraries do not advocate the ideas found in their collections. The presence of a magazine or book in a library does not indicate an endorsement of its contents by the library.

3. No one person should take the responsibility of labeling publications. No sizable group of persons would be likely to agree either on the types of material which should be labeled or the sources of information which should be regarded with suspicion. As a practical consideration, a librarian who labeled a book or magazine pro-communist might be sued for libel.

4. Labeling is an attempt to prejudice the reader, and as such, it is a censor's tool.

5. Labeling violates the spirit of the Library Bill of Rights.

6. Although we are all agreed that communism is a threat to the free world, if materials are labeled to pacify one group, there is no excuse for refusing to label any item in the library's collection. Because communism, fascism, or other authoritarianisms tend to suppress ideas and attempt to coerce individuals to conform to a specific ideology, American librarians must be opposed to such "isms." We are, then, anti-Communist, but we are also opposed to any other group which aims at closing any path to knowledge.
Adopted July 13, 1951, by the ALA Council.

4.   Freedom to Read Statement

The freedom to read is essential to our democracy. It is under attack. Private groups and public authorities in various parts of the country are working to remove books from sale, to censor textbooks, to label "controversial" books, to distribute lists of "objectionable" books or authors, and to purge libraries. These actions apparently rise from a view that our national tradition of free expression is no longer valid; that censorship and suppression are needed to avoid the subversion of politics and the corruption of morals. We, as citizens devoted to the use of books and as librarians and publishers responsible for disseminating them, wish to assert the public interest in the preservation of the freedom to read.

We are deeply concerned about these attempts at suppression. Most such attempts rest on a denial of the fundamental premise of democracy: that the ordinary citizen, by exercising his critical judgment, will accept the good and reject the bad. The censors, public and private, assume that they should determine what is good and what is bad for their fellow citizens.

We trust Americans to recognize propaganda, and to reject obscenity. We do not believe they need the help of censors to assist them in this task. We do not believe they are prepared to sacrifice their heritage of a free press in order to be "protected" against what others think may be bad for them. We believe they still favor free enterprise in ideas and expression.

We are aware, of course, that books are not alone in being subjected to efforts at suppression. We are aware that these efforts are related to a larger pattern of pressures being brought against education, the press, films, radio and television. The problem is not only one of actual censorship. The shadow of fear cast by these pressures leads, we suspect, to an even larger voluntary curtailment of expression by those who seek to avoid controversy.

Such pressure toward conformity is perhaps natural to a time of uneasy change and pervading fear. Especially when so many of our apprehensions are directed against an ideology, the expression of a dissident idea becomes a thing feared in itself, and we tend to move against it as against a hostile deed, with suppression.

And yet suppression is never more dangerous than in such a time of social tension. Freedom has given the United States the elasticity to endure strain. Freedom keeps open the path of novel and creative solutions, and enables change to come by choice. Every silencing of a heresy, every enforcement of an orthodoxy, diminishes the toughness and resilience of our society and leaves it the less able to deal with stress.

Now as always in our history, books are among our greatest instruments of freedom. They are almost the only means for making generally available ideas or manners of expression that can initially command only a small audience. They are the natural medium for the new idea and the untried voice from which come the original contributions to social growth. They are essential to the extended discussion which serious thought requires, and to the accumulation of knowledge and ideas into organized collections.

We believe that free communication is essential to the preservation of a free society and a creative culture. We believe that these pressures towards conformity present the danger of limiting the range and variety of inquiry and expression on which our democracy and our culture depend. We believe that every American community must jealously guard the freedom to publish and to circulate, in order to preserve its own freedom to read. We believe that publishers and librarians have a profound responsibility to give validity to that freedom to read by making it possible for the readers to choose freely from a variety of offerings.

The freedom to read is guaranteed by the Constitution. Those with faith in free men and will stand firm on these constitutional guarantees of essential rights and will exercise the responsibilities that accompany these rights.

We therefore affirm these propositions:

1. It is in the public interest for publishers and librarians to make available the widest diversity of views and expressions, including those which are unorthodox or unpopular with the majority.

Creative thought is by definition new, and what is new is different. The bearer of every new thought is a rebel until his idea is refined and tested. Totalitarian systems attempt to maintain themselves in power by the ruthless suppression of any concept which challenges the established orthodoxy. The power of a democratic system to adapt to change is vastly strengthened by the freedom of its citizens to choose widely from among conflicting opinions offered freely to them. To stifle every nonconformist idea at birth would mark the end of the democratic process. Furthermore, only through the constant activity of weighing and selecting can the democratic mind attain the strength demanded by times like these. We need to know not only what we believe but why we believe it.

2. Publishers and librarians do not need to endorse every idea or presentation contained in the books they make available. It would conflict with the public interest for them to establish their own political, moral or aesthetic views as the sole standard for determining what books should be published or circulated.

Publishers and librarians serve the educational process by helping to make available knowledge and ideas required for the growth of the mind and the increase of learning. They do not foster education by imposing as mentors the patterns of their own thought. The people should have the freedom to read and consider a broader range of ideas than those that may be held by any single librarian or publisher or government or church. It is wrong that what one man can read should be confined to what another thinks proper.

3. It is contrary to the public interest for publishers or librarians to determine the acceptability of a book solely on the basis of the personal history or political affiliations of the author.

A book should be judged as a book. No art or literature can flourish if it is to be measured by the political views or private lives of its creators. No society of free men can flourish which draws up lists of writers to whom it will not listen, whatever they may have to say.

4. The present laws dealing with obscenity should be vigorously enforced. Beyond that, there is no place in our society for extralegal efforts to coerce the taste of others, to confine adults to the reading matter deemed suitable for adolescents, or to inhibit the efforts of writers to achieve artistic expression.

To some, much of modern literature is shocking. But is not much of life itself shocking? We cut off literature at the source if we prevent serious artists from dealing with the stuff of life. Parents and teachers have a responsibility to prepare the young to meet the diversity of experiences in life to which they will be exposed, as they have a responsibility to help them learn to think critically for themselves. These are affirmative responsibilities, not to be discharged simply by preventing them from reading works for which they are not yet prepared. In these matters taste differs, and taste cannot be legislated; nor can machinery be devised which will suit the demands of one group without limiting the freedom of others. We deplore the catering to the immature, the retarded or the maladjusted taste. But those concerned with freedom have the responsibility of seeing to it that each individual book or publication, whatever its contents, price or method of distribution, is dealt with in accordance with due process of law.

5. *It is not in the public interest to force a reader to accept with any book the prejudgment of a label characterizing the book or author as subversive or dangerous.*

The idea of labeling presupposes the existence of individuals or groups with wisdom to determine by authority what is good or bad for the citizen. It presupposes that each individual must be directed in making up his mind about the ideas he examines. But Americans do not need others to do their thinking for them.

6. *It is the responsibility of publishers and librarians, as guardians of the people's freedom to read, to contest encroachments upon that freedom by individuals or groups seeking to impose their own standards or tastes upon the community at large.*

It is inevitable in the give and take of the democratic process that the political, the moral, or the aesthetic concepts of an individual or group will occasionally collide with those of another individual or group. In a free society each individual is free to determine for himself what he wishes to read, and each group is free to determine what it will recommend to its freely associated members. But no group has the right to take the law into its own hands, and to impose its own concept of politics or morality upon other members of a democratic society. Freedom is no freedom if it is accorded only to the accepted and the inoffensive.

7. *It is the responsibility of publishers and librarians to give full meaning to the freedom to read by providing books that enrich the quality of thought and expression. By the exercise of this affirmative responsibility, bookmen can demonstrate that the answer to a bad book is a good one, the answer to a bad idea is a good one.*

The freedom to read is of little consequence when expended on the trivial; it is frustrated when the reader cannot obtain matter fit for his purpose. What is needed is not only the absence of restraint, but the positive provision of opportunity for the people to read the best that has been thought and said. Books are the major channel by which the intellectual inheritance is handed down, and the principal means of its testing and growth. The defense of their freedom and integrity, and the enlargement of their service to society, requires of all bookmen the utmost of their faculties, and deserves of all citizens the fullest of their support.

We state these propositions neither lightly nor as easy generalizations. We here stake out a lofty claim for the value of books. We do so because we believe that they are good, possessed of enormous variety and usefulness, worthy of cherishing and keeping free. We realize that the application of these propositions may mean the dissemination of ideas and manners of expression that are repugnant to many persons. We do not state these propositions in the comfortable belief that what people read is unimportant. We believe rather that what people read is deeply important; that ideas can be dangerous; but that the suppression of ideas is fatal to a democratic society. Freedom itself is a dangerous way of life, but it is ours.

Adopted June 25, 1953, by the ALA Council.

Endorsed by:

AMERICAN LIBRARY ASSOCIATION   *Council, June 25, 1953*

AMERICAN BOOK PUBLISHERS COUNCIL   *Board of Directors, June 18, 1953*

Subsequently Endorsed by:

AMERICAN BOOKSELLERS ASSOCIATION   *Board of Directors*

BOOK MANUFACTURERS' INSTITUTE   *Board of Directors*

NATIONAL EDUCATION ASSOCIATION   *Commission for the Defense of Democracy through Education*

5.   School Library Bill of Rights

School libraries are concerned with generating understanding of American freedoms and with the preservation of these freedoms through the development of informed and responsible citizens. To this end the American Association of School Librarians reaffirms the *Library Bill of Rights* of the American Library Association and asserts that the responsibility of the school library is:

To provide materials that will enrich and support the curriculum, taking into consideration the varied interests, abilities, and maturity levels of the pupils served

To provide materials that will stimulate growth in factual knowledge, literary appreciation, aesthetic values, and ethical standards

To provide a background of information which will enable pupils to make intelligent judgments in their daily life

To provide materials on opposing sides of controversial issues so that young citizens may develop under guidance the practice of critical reading and thinking

To provide materials representative of the many religious, ethnic, and cultural groups and their contributions to our American heritage

To place principle above personal opinion and reason above prejudice in the selection of materials of the highest quality in order to assure a comprehensive collection appropriate for the users of the library.

Adopted by the American Association of School Libraries, a division of the American Library Association, and endorsed by the Council of the American Library Association, July 1955.

6.　　　How Libraries and Schools Can Resist Censorship

Libraries of all sizes and types have been under increasing pressures from persons who wish to use the library as an instrument of their own tastes and views. Such individuals and groups are demanding the exclusion or removal of books to which they object or the inclusion of a higher proportion of books that support their views. Similar attacks have been made on schools in connection with books used in their programs. In view of this fact, it seems desirable to set forth a few basic principles that may help librarians, trustees, and school administrators in preserving the freedom and professional integrity of their institutions.

The problem differs somewhat between the public library, with a responsibility to the public to present as wide a spectrum of significant reading matter as its budget can afford, and the school library, whose collections are designed to support the educational objectives of the school. In both, however, there is involved the freedom of the school or the library to meet its professional responsibilities to the whole community.

Every library or school should take certain measures to clarify its policies and establish its community relations. These steps should be taken without regard to any attack or prospect of attack. They will put the institution in a firm and clearly defined position if its book policies are ever called into question.

As a normal operating procedure, every library, and the administration responsible for it, should establish certain principles.

1. There should be a definite book selection policy. This should be in written form and approved by the board of trustees, the school board, or other administrative authority. It should be stated clearly and should be un-

derstood by members of the staff. This policy should apply to other materials equally, i.e., films, records, magazines, and pamphlets.

2. A file recording the basis for decision should be kept for titles likely to be questioned or apt to be considered controversial.

3. There should be a clearly defined method for handling complaints. Any complaint should be required to be in writing, and the complainant should be identified properly before the complaint is considered. Action should be deferred until full consideration by appropriate administrative authority.

4. There should be continuing efforts to establish lines of communication to assure mutual understanding with civic, religious, educational, and political bodies.

5. Newspapers of the community should be informed of policies governing book selection and use. Purposes and services of the library should be interpreted through a continuing public relations program, as should the use of books in the school.

6. Participation in local civic organizations and in community affairs is desirable. The library and the school are key centers of the community; the librarian and school administrator should be known publicly as community leaders.

If an attack does come, remember the following:

1. Remain calm. Don't confuse noise with substance. Most attacks come from small groups of people who have little community backing. Time after time the American people have shown that, given the facts, they will back solidly the responsible exercise of professional freedom by teachers and librarians and that they will insist on protecting their own freedom to read. Insist on the deliberate handling of the complaint under previously established rules. Treat complainants with dignity, courtesy, and good humor.

2. Take immediate steps to assure that the full facts surrounding a complaint are known to the administration. The school librarian should go through the principal to the superintendent and the school board; the public librarian, to the board of trustees or to the appropriate community administration official; the college or university librarian, to the president and through him to the board of trustees. Full, written information should be presented, giving the nature of the problem or complaint and identifying the source.

3. Seek the support of the local press immediately. The freedom to read and the freedom of the press go hand in hand.

4. Inform local civic organizations of the facts and enlist their support where possible.

5. Defend the principles of the freedom to read and the professional responsibility of teachers and librarians rather than the individual book. The laws governing obscenity, subversive material, and other questionable matter

are subject to interpretation by the courts. The responsibility for removal of any book from public access should rest with this established process. The responsibility for the use of books in the schools must rest with those responsible for the educational objectives being served.

6. The ALA Intellectual Freedom Committee and other appropriate national and state committees concerned with intellectual freedom should be informed of the nature of the problem. Even though each effort at censorship must be met at the local level, there is often value in the support and assistance of agencies outside the area which have no personal involvement. They often can cite parallel cases and suggest methods of meeting an attack. Similar aid in cases affecting the use of books in the schools can be obtained from the Commission on Professional Rights and Responsibilities of the National Education Association.

Every librarian should be familiar with certain basic documents which have been prepared by the American Library Association and represent the position of this national organization of more than 26,000 librarians. Copies of each of these may be obtained by writing the American Library Association, 50 East Huron Street. [Chicago, Illinois 60611].

Adopted February 1, 1962, by the ALA Council.

7.   Citizen's Request for Reconsideration of a Book

Author .... Hardcover .... Paperback ....

Title ....

Publisher (if known) ....

Request initiated by ....

Telephone .... Address ....

City .... Zone ....

Complainant represents .... himself

                     .... (name organization) ....

                     .... (identify other group) ....

1. To what in the book do you object? (Please be specific; cite pages.)
....

2. What do you feel might be the result of reading this book? ......
....

3. For what age group would you recommend this book? ....

4. Is there anything good about this book? ....

5. Did you read the entire book? .... What parts? ....
....

6. Are you aware of the judgment of this book by literary critics? ....

7. What do you believe is the theme of this book? ....
....
8. What would you like your school to do about this book?
.... do not assign it to my child
.... withdraw it from all students as well as from my child
.... send it back to the English department office for reevaluation
9. In its place, what book of equal literary quality would you recommend that would convey as valuable a picture and perspective of
our civilization? ....
....
Signature of Complainant

The National Council of Teachers of English, *The Students'
Right to Read* (Champaign, Ill.: The Council, 1962), p. 17.

8. Intellectual Freedom in Libraries

A. Preamble

The following statement of policy was developed by the
Intellectual Freedom Committee of the California Library Association and
the Book Selection Policies Committee of the School Library Association of
California. These professional associations are directly concerned with the
freedom of all members of a democratic society to read what they will in the
course of making the social, educational, and political judgments on which
that society is based. Without such freedom the very fabric of democracy is
in danger. There is evidence that books and libraries are the chief bastion
against the pressures toward conformity which are in large part already
overwhelming the motion picture, radio and television, and the press. Only
in libraries can the interested student easily find record of the past, and only
in libraries can the interested citizen hope to find all the relevant facts concerning current controversial issues. It is appropriate that librarians should
deem their freedom, and that of their libraries, of the utmost importance
to the continued existence of democracy.

B. Authority

Through their respective Boards of Directors the Associations have empowered the Intellectual Freedom Committee of the California Library Association (Resolution passed at meeting held at Long
Beach, on 28 October 1958) and the Book Selection Policies Committee of
the School Library Association of California (Resolution passed at meeting
held at Riverside, on 7 November 1958) to act in their behalf in all four
areas of concern described below. These areas of concern constitute continuing responsibilities of the two Committees, acting separately or together,
until this Statement of Policy is amended or revoked.

C. Areas of Concern

1. The Associations are concerned with watching for proposed legislation at the state, local, and school district level which might place library collections in jeopardy, or which might restrict, prejudice, or otherwise interfere with the selection, acquisition, or other professional activities of librarians.

The Committees are instructed to write letters to and talk with legislators and administrators to present the Associations' point of view, and to appear before legislative and administrative committees in the interest of preserving freedom of the press and the right to read.

2. The Associations are also concerned with legislation at the state, local, and school district level which tends to strengthen the position of libraries and other media of communication as instruments of knowledge and culture in a free society.

The Committees are instructed to watch for legislation in the general field of the communication of knowledge and ideas which the Associations might desirably support as being beneficial to the whole concept embodied in the phrase "Freedom to Read." The Committees are instructed to inform the Association memberships of such pending legislation, to present their recommendations, and to tender the Associations' support to such legislation.

3. The Associations are concerned with proposed or actual restrictions imposed by individuals, voluntary committees, or administrative authority on library materials or on the selection judgments, order procedures, or administrative practices of librarians.

The Committees are instructed, at will or on request of either party to a controversy, to (a) determine the facts; (b) develop a statement of the Associations' position in relation to this statement of policy; (c) present the Associations' position to all interested parties, including the Press, when, in the Committees' judgment, this seems wise or necessary.

4. The Associations believe that every library, in order to strengthen its own selection process, and to provide an objective basis for the evaluation of that process, should develop an official statement of policy for the selection of library materials.

The Committees are instructed to collect existing selection policies from all types of libraries, to promote their development and official adoption by libraries not yet having them, and to develop sample prototypes of selection policies for the guidance of librarians writing such policies.

Adopted by the California Library Association and the School Library Association of California, November 1958.

BIBLIOGRAPHY

American Library Association, Coordinating Committee on Revision of
Public Library Standards, *Public Library Service: A
Guide to Evaluation, with Minimum Standards* (Chi-
cago: The Association, 1956).

Asheim, Lester, "Not Censorship but Selection," *Wilson Library Bulletin*, 28 (September 1953), 63-7.

Berelson, Bernard, "The Myth of Library Impartiality," *Wilson Library
Bulletin*, 13 (October 1938), 87-90.

Berninghausen, David K., "The History of the ALA Intellectual Freedom Committee," *Wilson Library Bulletin*, 27 (June
1953), 813-17.

Broderick, Dorothy M., "Problem Nonfiction," *Library Journal*, 87 (October 1, 1962), 3373-8.

Bundy, Mary Lee, "Metropolitan Public Library Use," *Wilson Library
Bulletin*, 41 (May 1967), 950-61.

Carnovsky, Leon, "Measurement of Public Library Book Collections,"
Library Trends, 1 (April 1953), 462-70.

Carter, Mary Duncan and Bonk, Wallace John, *Building Library Collections,* Third Edition (New York: Scarecrow Press, 1969).

Clor, Harry M., *Obscenity and Public Morality: Censorship in a Liberal Society* (Chicago: University of Chicago Press, 1969).

Danton, J. Periam, ed., *The Climate of Book Selection* (Berkeley: University of California, School of Librarianship, 1959).

De Grazia, Edward, *Censorship Landmarks* (New York: R. R. Bowker Company, 1969).

De Grazia, Edward, "Defending the Freedom to Read in the Courts," *ALA Bulletin,* 59 (June 1965), 507-15.

Fiske, Marjorie, *Book Selection and Censorship* (Berkeley: University of California Press, 1959).

Goldhor, Herbert, "Are the Best Books the Most Read?," *Library Quarterly,* 29 (October 1959), 251-5.

Haines, Helen E., *Living With Books: The Art of Book Selection.* Second Edition (New York: Columbia University Press, 1950).

Leigh, Robert D., *The Public Library in the United States* (New York: Columbia University Press, 1950).

McCoy, Ralph E., *Freedom of the Press: An Annotated Bibliography* (Carbondale: Southern Illinois University Press, 1968).

McDiarmid, Errett Weir, *The Library Survey: Problems and Methods* (Chicago: American Library Association, 1940).

Molz, Kathleen, "Public Custody of the High Pornography," *American Scholar,* 36 (Winter 1966-67) 93-103.

Moon, Eric, ed., *Book Selection and Censorship in the Sixties* (New York: R. R. Bowker Company, 1969).

New Jersey Committee for the Right to Read, *A Survey of New Jersey Psychiatrists and Psychologists Pertaining to the Proscription by Legislation of Sexually Oriented Publications for Persons Under 18 Years* (Caldwell: The Committee, 1967).

Ranganathan, S. R. and Gopinath, M. A., *Library Book Selection* (New York: Asia Publishing House, 1967).

Rembar, Charles, *The End of Obscenity: The Trials of Lady Chatterley, Tropic of Cancer, and Fanny Hill* (New York: Random House, 1968).

Williams, Edwin E., "Surveying Library Collections," In *Library Surveys*, edited by Maurice F. Tauber and Irlene R. Stephens, (New York: Columbia University Press, 1967), pp. 23-45.

Wisconsin Free Library Commission, *Proceedings of the Eighth Institute on Public Library Management* (Madison: The Commission, 1961).

INDEX

Additions, 59-61
Adult book selection policy, 33-50
Age of reader, 18-19
American Association of State Librar-
ies, 69n
American Civil Liberties Union, 68-9
*American Library Association News-
letter on Intellectual Freedom*, 67n
American Library Association Policies,
66n
"Are the Best Books the Most Read?,"
62n
Arrangement, The, 14
Art books, 37
Asheim, Lester, 12, 22
Audience, Unlimited, 67
Audience Unlimited News, 76

*Basic List of Adult Books for Branches
of the D.C. Public Library*, 61n
Berelson, Bernard, 16
Berninghausen, David K., 72n

Bill of Rights, Library, 18, 66, 70, 72,
82-3
Biography, 37
Blackshear, Orrilla, 19-20, 78
Blanshard, Paul, 15
Blue Book of John Birch Society, 16
Bonk, Carter and, 14, 62
Book Selection and Censorship, 13n,
78n
Book selection and intellectual free-
dom, 11-23
Books as news, 16-17
Bookstock, 59-61
Breadth of book selection, 36
Broderick, Dorothy, 14, 20
Bundy, Mary Lee, 17n, 59n

Calories Don't Count, 20
Carnovsky, Leon, 56
Carter and Bonk, 14, 62
Censorship, How Libraries and Schools
Can Resist, 89-91

Censorship and the Teacher, 69
Censorship Bulletin, 76
Censorship on local level, 80
Censorship Today, 76
Checklist method, 57
Chemistry, 37-8
Children's book selection, 52-4
Children's Catalog, 57
Circulation, 59-61
Civil service, 38
Climate of Book Selection, The, 78n, 79n
Closed shelves and locked cases, 17-18
Committee on Intellectual Freedom of the American Library Association, 65-6, 73
Communism, 38
Communist Manifesto, The, 16
Court briefs, 80

Danton, J. Periam, 78, 79n
Davis, Adele, 19
"Dayton Tests Selection Policy Against Election Campaign Books," 16n
"Defending the Freedom to Read in the Courts," 23n
De Grazia, Edward, 22, 23n
Depth of book selection, 36
Dianetics, 19
Dictionary of American Slang, 21
Drugs, 39
Duplication of selection, 36

Economics, 39
Education, 39
Elementary school, 53
Evaluating the policy, 55-63
Evergreen Review, 68
Expert opinion, 58

Fiction, 39-41
Fine arts, 41
Fiske, Marjorie, 13, 78
Folk and fairy literature, 53
Foreign language, 41-2
Freedom of Inquiry, Supporting the Library Bill of Rights, 77n
Freedom-to-Read Bulletin, 76
Freedom to Read Statement, 84-8
Freedom to Teach—Freedom to Learn, 69

Friedenberg, Edgar Z., 19

Gaines, Ervin J., 19, 77
Genealogy, 42
Geography and travel, 42
Geology, 43
Goldhor, Herbert, 62
Gross size of library, 56
Grove Press, 68

Haines, H.E., 14
Haley, J. Evetts, 16
Health and medicine, 19-20
History, 43
local, 44
"History of the ALA Intellectual Freedom Committee, The," 72n
Hubbard, L. Ronald, 19
Human relations, 53

Illinois Freedom to Read Committee, 67
Information kits, 74
Intellectual freedom, book selection and, 11-23
Intellectual freedom, professional activity in behalf of, 71-81
Intellectual Freedom in Libraries, 92-3

John Birch Society, *Blue Book,* 16
Junior high school students through the eighth grade, 53

Krug, Judith F., 65

Labeling, Statement on, 16, 83-4
Language, 43
Last Temptation of Christ, 78
Law, 44
Legislative activity, 78-80
Leigh, Robert D., 58
Library Bill of Rights, 18, 66, 70, 72, 82-3
Library Functions of the States, 69n
Library science, 44
Library Survey, The, 56n
Library Surveys, 56n
Literature, 44
Locked cases, closed shelves and, 17-18
Long Island Intellectual Freedom Committee, 67
Loyalty Programs, Resolution on, 83

Lyman, Helen H., 78

McDiarmid, Errett Weir, 56
Mathematics, 44-5
"Measurement of Public Library Book Collections," 56n
Medicine, 45-6
 health and, 19-20
Mein Kampf, 16
"Metropolitan Public Library Use," 17n, 59n
Mills, Forrest, 61
Monypenny, Philip, 69
Moore, Everett T., 75
Mosher, Fredric J., 79
Music, 46
"Myth of Library Impartiality, The," 16

National Council of Teachers of English, 69
National Decency Reporter, 77
National Education Association's Commission on Professional Rights and Responsibilities, 69
New Jersey Committee for the Right to Read, 67
Newsletter on Intellectual Freedom, 13, 19, 74-6, 77, 78
Newsletters, 74
NODL Newsletter, 76-7
"Not Censorship but Selection," 12n

Obscenity and Censorship, 68n
Obscenity and pornography, 13-14
Obscenity, the Law and the English Teacher, 69
On-shelf status, 59
Opinion, expert, 58
Ownby, Donald W., 58

Peyton Place, 16, 17
Philosophy, 46
Physics, 46
Policies and Procedures for Selection of School Library Materials, 25n
Political science, 47
Politics, 16
Pornography, obscenity and, 13-14
Preschool, 52

Printing and publishing, 47
"Problem Nonfiction," 14n, 20n
Proceedings of the Eighth Institute on Public Library Management, 78n
Professional associations, role of, 64-70
Pseudoscientific books, 47
Psychology, 47-8
Public Library Catalog, 57
Public Library in the United States, 58n
Public Library Service, 24
Publishing, printing and, 47
Putnam, Carleton, 17

Race and Reason, 17
Racine Public Library, 61
Ranganathan, S.R., 14
Range of book selection, 36
Reader's Right, 76
Reconsideration of a Book, Citizen's Request for, 91-2
Religion, 15-16, 48-9, 54
Resolution on Loyalty Programs, 83
Role of professional associations and state library agencies, 64-70

Sample selection policies, 32-54
School Library Bill of Rights, 88-9
Selection policy
 for adults, 33-50
 art, 37
 biography, 37
 chemistry, 37-8
 for children, 52-4
 civil service, 38
 communism, 38
 drugs, 39
 economics, 39
 education, 39
 evaluation, 55-63
 fiction, 39-41
 fine arts, 41
 foreign language, 41-2
 genealogy, 42
 general guidelines, 35-6
 geography and travel, 42
 geology, 43
 history, 43, 44
 human relations, 53-4
 language, 43

law, 44
library science, 44
literature, 44
mathematics, 44-5
medicine, 45-6
music, 46
philosophy, 46
physics, 46
political science, 47
printing and publishing, 47
pseudoscientific books, 47
psychology, 47-8
religion, 48-9, 54
sample, 32-54
sex, 49, 54
social sciences, 50
sociology, 50
terms of reference, 36-7
use of books, 35
writing a, 24-31
for young adults, 50-2
Senior High School Library Catalog, 57
"Setting the Stage in California," 79n
Sex, 49, 54
Sex education, 14-15
Shelves, closed, and locked cases, 17-18
Size of library, gross, 56
Social sciences, 50

Sociology, 50
Standards for Library Functions at the State Level, 69
State library agencies, role of, 64-70
Stephens, Irlene R., 56n
Student's Right to Read, The, 69
Survey of New Jersey Psychiatrists and Psychologists Pertaining to the Proscription by Legislation of Sexually Oriented Publications for Persons Under 18 Years, 67n
"Surveying Library Collections," 56n

Taller, Herman, 20
Tauber, Maurice F., 56n
Texan Looks at Lyndon, A, 16
Travel, geography and, 42
Tropic of Cancer, 78, 80

Use, evidence of, 61-3

Valley of the Dolls, 14

Webster's Third New International Dictionary, 13n
Widmer, Kingsley, 69
Williams, Edwin E., 56
Workshops and institutes, 77

Young adult book selection policy, 50-2